Haunted Gettysburg

Carol Starr & Mark Sarro

4880 Lower Valley Road • Atglen, PA 19310

Gettysburg

Haunted Gettysburg

Cover photo © Scott Butcher, www.scottbutcher.com.

All photos unless otherwise noted were captured by authors Carol Starr and Mark Sarro.

Ouija is a registered trademark of Parker Brother's Games.

Designed by Stephanie Daugherty
Type set in Demon Night/New Baskerville BT/Gil Sans

ISBN: 978-0-7643-3310-1
Printed in China

Published by Schiffer Publishing, Ltd.
4880 Lower Valley Road
Atglen, PA 19310
Phone: (610) 593-1777; Fax: (610) 593-2002
E-mail: Info@schifferbooks.com
Web: www.schifferbooks.com

For our complete selection of fine books on this and related subjects, please visit our website at www.schifferbooks.com. You may also write for a free catalog.

Schiffer Publishing's titles are available at special discounts for bulk purchases for sales promotions or premiums. Special editions, including personalized covers, corporate imprints, and excerpts, can be created in large quantities for special needs. For more information, contact the publisher.

We are always looking for people to write books on new and related subjects. If you have an idea for a book, please contact us at proposals@schifferbooks.com.

ACKNOWLEDGMENTS

Carol Starr

I want to thank quite a few people in helping me with this book. To Dinah Roseberry from Schiffer Publishing; I can't thank you enough for all your help, patience and guidance. It was so appreciated. To Chester County Paranormal Research Society (CCPRS) members for their support. We are a family and being a part of this group is a dream come true for me.

To Joe and Karen Svehla from Ghostly Images. You both went above and beyond with your kindness and generosity as I was working on this book. You opened many doors for us in Gettysburg (literally) and gave me the inspiration that I needed to write. Thanks Joe for setting an example with you own wonderful books. To Bob Michaels from Ghostly Images for all your wisdom, stories, and support.

To Laurie Hull and Rich Hickman from Delaware County Paranormal Research. You both contributed so much to this book; thank you for sharing your stories and pictures with me.

To my family and friends, Thank you for your support and encouragement throughout the past couple of years.

And last but not least, thank you to my co-author and friend, Mark Sarro. You have given me the confidence and guidance that I needed to make this endeavor successful.

Mark Sarro

This book would have not been possible if it had not been for the direct contributions of:

Laurie Hull and Rich Hickman from Delaware County Paranormal Research; the members of CCPRS who participated in the investigations and research (Bob, Kim, Mary, Kat, Carol, Ken, Melissa, and Isaac); Robbin Van Pelt for her contributions to the book and to the field of Paranormal Research as a whole. It has been a great pleasure working with you over the years.

To Joe and Karen Svehla and Bob Michaels from Ghostly Images Tours. I have greatly enjoyed working with you and welcome your friendship. Dinah Roseberry, your continued patience and support has helped keep me going and seeing it through until the end. Thank you!

To Carol Starr, my co-author and friend. We worked hard on this book and it was worth it. Thank you!

Contents

Gettysburg

Haunted Gettysburg

FORWARD

Although I have only known Mark and Carol a relatively short time, I feel that I have known them a lot longer. Maybe it is because we have the same roots where our interest in the supernatural is concerned. I became interested as a young boy growing up in Baltimore across the street from a haunted church. At age six, Mark was living in a home that had once been a funeral parlor. Carol's venture into the unknown began at age six also, when she witnessed a full-body apparition at her Aunt's home. Once you have had your first encounter, there is no turning back!

Our paths crossed when Mark and Carol came to visit the Jennie Wade House Museum along with Mark's investigative team, Chester County Paranormal Research Society (CCPRS). As Manager of Ghostly Images of Gettysburg Ghost Tours and, at that time, Historical Interpreter for the Museum, it was my responsibility to work with their team by arranging their visit. The investigation that they conducted was, by far, the most thorough and professional that had been done at that truly haunted house.

What was even more impressive for me was the time and effort that they put into their presentation of the evidence they collected. They presented us with every minute detail including audio, video, still photograph, personal experiences, etc., all on computer disc.

Mark and Carol have proven to be not only true professionals in the supernatural field, but also good friends. With the attention to every detail and the work effort they have shown, there is no doubt in my mind that the manuscript that they are presenting to the public will be a quality work worthy of their consideration.

To Mark and Carol—Thanks for your friendship; thanks for your interest in Gettysburg and good luck in your new endeavor.

~ Joe Svehla
Manager, Ghostly Images Tours and
Author of the Ghostly Images
Catch the Spirits series

Introduction

Carol Starr

My first trip to Gettysburg was way back in junior high school on a class trip. At that time, I don't think I gave it much thought—other than getting a day away from school—but I do remember the beautiful rolling hills and farms and the peaceful little town. I think I knew then that I would be drawn back to Gettysburg time and time again. At first, in search of history and answers to some of my historical questions, and then finally, coming back to seek out spirits of those who perished during those bloody three days of battle.

Within this book, I will have a bit of the famous history, but mostly I'll talk about my personal experiences in the past few years with the soldiers that are no longer of this earth. Whether you believe in ghosts or not, Gettysburg is rich with history... and something else, something unfinished, something somewhat sad. I hope you enjoy my stories and also those that have been contributed by others.

Mark Sarro

Gettysburg has to be one of most beautiful, yet sad places that I have been to. To stand at the top of Little Round Top and look out over the rolling hills and down through the Slaughter Pen and then to Devil's Den and even off to Triangular Field and the Wheatfield, you realize just how beautiful and peaceful this place is. In that instant, to close your eyes and imagine what it must have been like during those three days of July in 1863. The men who fought and died there, in total over 50,000 dead within those three days. To think that a place as peaceful as the Wheatfield was once so over run with the dead and dying that not a single piece of ground could be seen throughout the entire field. It is horrific to think about, yet the course of events in those three days would change the shape and direction that our country would ultimately go. I find it awe inspiring to think of these things. No matter how many times I go back and how many times that I stand at the top of Little Round Top and look out; I can't help but think of the struggles of that time.

The history of Gettysburg is what initially drew me; in my youth this was the place of a field trip and place to learn of the history and to learn of the brave and valiant men who fought and died there. The ghosts and spirits were not something that would come until much later. It really wasn't until about four years or more ago that I first visited Gettysburg in pursuit of the spirits that roam. This book is filled with the collective experiences of myself, my friend and co-author, Carol Starr, members of CCPRS, and our esteemed friends and colleagues. I invite you to experience these events through the eyes of the investigator as we take you to the heart of an investigation in some of the famous, and not so famous, places in Gettysburg.

My hope is to enlighten, entertain, and educate you regarding these kinds of experiences. I imagine that you are reading this book because in some way you already believe. I encourage you to go and see and visit these places that we write about. Go and experience firsthand the beauty of the national parks and the charm of historic Gettysburg. Visit the museums, take the tours, and enjoy the rich history that is so important to our country.

The spirits of Gettysburg are now just as important and vital as the history itself. You never know when you may have that random encounter. It may be in the park, on the street, in your hotel room, and usually when you least expect it. They are not to be feared, but they all, in their own ways, have a story to be told and are looking and hoping for someone to stop and listen. This book is a mere glimpse at the hundreds, or even thousands, of experiences had by individuals in Gettysburg.

Here now, we intend to share some of these encounters with you, as they happened and through the eyes of those who experienced them.

Enjoy!

CHAPTER 1

SPANGLER'S SPRING

Mark Sarro

A BRIEF HISTORY

Both Union and Confederate soldiers met here under a truce to drink the water on those hot July days in 1863.

Spangler's Spring, like many of the sites in Gettysburg, would too see its share of battle. On the afternoon of July 2, 1863, the Union soldiers of the 12th Army Corps were ordered away to assist Union soldiers at the nearby Peach Orchard. Under the cover of darkness, General Steuart and his men of the Confederate Army came upon the abandoned works. Meanwhile,

Confederate troops that ran adjacent to Steuart's men ran into General Greene's men and fighting broke out. Fighting continued to go on until Steuart and his men held back the advancing Union troops.

Everything quieted down after 11pm that evening, but Steuart had the sense that the Union troops would soon strike again. A counter-attack began at 4am as the soldiers from the 12th Army Corps returned. Steuart and his men were trapped in the knoll at the spring. The

While walking through this area, several investigators reported smelling a foul stench.

battle raged on, and at the peak of battle, two Union regiments, the 2nd Massachusetts and the 27th Indiana, were ordered to go in where Steuart and his men were pinned down.

Lieutenant Colonel Charles Mudge of the 2nd Massachusetts knew that this was going to be bloody and told his troops, "Boys, it is murder, but these are our orders!" They went in and Mudge and his troops were hit by musket fire on three sides. Mudge would not survive the battle.

The battle had been raging on for hours, and finally, Steuart and his men were ordered to retreat and reform with the division. Steuart had lost 189 of his 400 men from the 1st Maryland Battalion, and the 1st and 3rd North Carolina regiments of his brigade had lost nearly half of their men. The Union regained control of Spangler's Spring on July 3, 1863. Hundreds of soldiers had died on these grounds. The surviving Union soldiers quickly began to bury the dead.

Mark Sarro
THE MASS GRAVE

On the afternoon of November 11, 2007, CCPRS members, Carol, Kat, Kim, and I set out to visit Spangler Spring. We had been making our rounds to the various sites throughout the park when, while we were unloading equipment at one of the locations, we were approached by two men from the car next to us.

"What do you have there?" the older man asked me.

"That's an anemometer; it's used for measuring wind speed and wind chill," I replied as I held it up for him to see. I had just pulled the device from my equipment case and was attaching my digital compass to my waist when he asked me another question.

"Are you guys like those Ghost Hunters on TV?" he asked.

"Kind of, something like that…" I replied hesitantly. Carol and Kim were standing to my side and gathering their equipment as well and both glanced at me as I answered.

"That's very cool. Have you guys been to the mass grave?" he asked.

"No, I'm not familiar with it. What are you talking about?" I asked. Mass graves. He had our attention.

"It's the grave associated with the battle of Spangler's Spring at the top of the hill off behind the 2nd Maryland monument," he stated.

"We'll have to go check that out," said Carol with interest.

"Yeah, we were just there a little while ago. You can't miss it; the area is marked with a Confederate flag."

"Alright, great! We will definitely stop by to see it," I stated.

"Happy hunting!" the man replied as he walked away with his friend.

I turned to Carol and said, "We will definitely have to go to see what that's all about!"

"Yeah, absolutely. I have never been there." she replied.

"Me neither!" added Kim.

We had finished checking out the area we were in and decided to make our way over to Spangler's Spring. Parking the car, we got out and geared up with our equipment. We were first going to check out the spring and then try and make our way to find where the mass grave was supposed to be. The spring itself was fairly open. We were facing it to our right and there was a line of trees to the left. The hill sloped up steeply to the right and a line of trees ran along the top of the hill. There were several large rocks strewn out amongst the trees and we began to make our way across the road and into the land where the spring was located. The weather was fairly mild that day and was in the low 50's. We walked all the way back through the field and trees along the edge of the hill to our right. Once we'd gone out as far as we could to a line of trees directly in front of us, we decided to turn around. We had been taking photographs and monitoring the EMF and temperature as we walked in the area. As we began to slowly make our way back to the car, I suddenly stopped.

(Please see the Equipment Explanation section in the back of the book to find out about EMF meters and how they function.)

A Smell Worth Remembering

"It smells like something is rotting." I spoke aloud.

"Does anyone else smell that?" I asked. Carol came closer to me and tried to see if she could smell it too.

"Yeah, I do. Where is that coming from?" She asked.

"I don't know," I replied. "It just kind of came out of nowhere."

"Maybe an animal died or something?" Kim suggested.

"It could be, but it seems to be isolated in this area!" We were in an open area on flat ground with lots of leaves on the ground.

"Maybe it's just rotting leaves," Kat remarked.

"I don't know, it could be." I knelt down to the ground in the exact area where I was standing and began to take heavy breaths of the ground and air around me. "It doesn't smell like leaves or anything from the ground. It's strange, I don't smell it down here." I stood back up and turned and looked around behind me and all over the surrounding area. "I don't know what it could be. It seems like it has already passed." I continued to look about me to see if anything could be seen.

"I don't smell it anymore," Carol said and Kim agreed that the smell was now gone.

"Whatever it was, it seemed to pass," I stated. It was very peculiar how quickly the smell had come and gone.

I had experienced something like that before during an investigation at a cemetery where something seemed to be following us. I didn't immediately jump to the conclusion that whatever this was had been paranormal, but I had to speculate at the possibility. It is quite common for strange smells to be had in areas of extreme paranormal activity. Phantom smells can happen as often as things being seen or heard. It's all the more reason why we are careful not to pollute the environment with heavy colognes or perfumes during an investigation. In fact, it is one of our protocols that all perfumes and colognes are banned during investigations for that very reason.

We had made it back to the car and it was now time to try and find the area of the mass grave. It was supposedly just up the hill and to the right, on the grounds directly above where Spangler Spring stood. We got in the car and began to drive slowly up the hill. We were paying special attention to the monuments, looking for the 2nd Maryland.

Kim was the one who spotted it. "Look, its right there!"

We pulled the car over and got out and started in the direction of the monument. Looking around behind it, towards the near area, we saw that the woods lined the roads just beyond the monuments. We had come across a small clearing, where you had to step down and into it. There were downed trees set up in an almost square pattern.

"Look! There's the flag!" Carol pointed to the ground in front of us as she spoke. I looked and there it was—a small Confederate flag stuck into the ground in the area of the trees. As I stepped into the area, I began to monitor the temperature and EMF readings.

".2, .4, .7," I said as I read the meter. I slowly turned to face the others. Carol stepped down into the area with me, and Kim was right behind her. Kat decided to go around and stand farther back towards the line of trees to our right. I sat down on one of the downed trees and Carol sat down to my left.

A Chill From the Grave

"I can feel cold creeping up my legs," Carol said as she turned towards me.

I looked down at the EMF meter that I'd sat down on my leg. ".9, 1.3, 1.5," I said as the meter was raising. I lowered my right hand down to my side and opened it out to feel the air around me. "It is colder all around on my right side."

"Yeah, I feel it moving up on me…" Carol added.

"The temperature on my compass is dropping." I watched the numbers slowly move downward.

"Oh wow, look! I can see my breath now!" Carol said, excitement in her voice, for this was a real find.

I turned to look at her and could see the breath coming out of her mouth. I began to breath heavy to see if I could see my own breath and I could. The cold was surrounding us and it was apparent that something was happening. Kat stood motionless with her back towards us as she faced out towards the trees.

"Kat! Are you alright?" I called out.

"Yeah…" She said slowly. "It's just… I get a sense that they are all over here." She

This marks the entrance to what is to be believed a mass grave.

motioned with her hand and turned around towards us. "I feel like they are here, they are all over this area… It's heavy and very sad," she said.

Kat was a sensitive and could feel, see, and interpret phenomena under the right conditions.

"The cold is all around us. I can feel it from my head to my to toes!" I continued, the wonder of it evident in my voice.

"Yeah, it's running all through me!" Carol said.

"It's almost too much… I don't know if I can take it!" Kat says, as she begins to make her way past us and back up to the road. I continued to sit in amazement at how cold it was and how quickly it seemed to consume us. It was heavy and seemed to be in our direct area. The sun was shining bright and it was a mild day. I couldn't believe the dramatic change in the environment around us. I continued to monitor the meter sitting on my lap.

"1.2, 1.5," I said again. The cold began to make me shiver. My legs began to tremble as I felt the cold seep deeper within me. Carol then stood up and Kim and had already began making her way back to the monuments and car. I still couldn't believe what was going on. We had no video or audio recorder running and it was killing me to know that this was happening and we had no way to prove it other than

a few photos that Carol had taken with her camera. But I realized that I, too, should move and not stay there much longer.

I grabbed the meter and stood up. Immediately, I felt the cold fall down around me and it instantly felt warmer upon standing. I started to step away from the area and looked at the meter. .4, .5, .2, my meter read as the readings dropped. I stepped over the downed tree,

This area is located behind the 2nd Maryland Monument and is believed to be the grave site of many confederate soldiers.

CCPRS investigators felt an eerie cold sensation creepinga up their legs while inside the log formation.

and closer back towards the monument did the warmth fully return and I no longer felt the cold as I did just ten to fifteen feet behind me in the area where the flag was. For the next few minutes we didn't say anything to each other. We all stood there in the area of the monuments and gathered our thoughts. It was an intense experience that we were all still digesting. I was truly astonished. I thought it was an amazing experience that we shared that day.

Carol Starr

This was the first time that I had been in this area of the battlefield, so we were excited to receive directions to the Mass Grave from some fellow visitors as we were unloading the car.

After we were geared up, we started walking towards the actual spring. There were leaves on the ground and it was a beautiful fall day. As we walked further back from the spring we split up and started to monitor our instruments. As I was walking, I was checking my EMF meter. Standing perfectly still, I watched my meter go from 0 to 2.7, 2.9, and up; then after a few moments, go back down to 0.

It felt as if there were waves of activity walking past us, or even through us. We also experienced a smell of rotting flesh or death, but though we searched around for a source to the smell, we couldn't find anything and it left very quickly.

up, and out of the area. The warmth was returning to my legs and face and I could no longer see my breath.

Turning around, I stood at the top of the small incline to look down into the area again. I had to stop and take it in for a moment and try to make sense of what had just happened. Even if this had not been the mass grave, something had just happened and we all experienced it together. No sooner did I step out from the line of the trees

Later, we started to walk towards the woods, and about 100 yards in, we noticed a small Confederate flag stuck in the ground. This area was square and surrounded by logs. The center of this area was sunken down. As I stepped into the square, I suddenly felt a coldness creep up my legs. It felt like icy hands working their way up my body. My EMF meter started to spike with high numbers.

My co-author and investigator, Mark Sarro, climbed into the square and sat down. Within minutes, he reported a sudden coldness creeping up his legs and he, too, described icy hands holding onto his legs.

The temperature inside the square started to drop. We started to see our breaths. Something was there and trying to get our attention. We could hear noises coming from the woods. Could this be the battle raging so close to Spangler Spring?

As we departed the area, the coldness went away and everything was back to normal. I checked with someone who knows the history of area well and was told that there is speculation that there was indeed a mass grave located there where Confederate soldiers were buried.

It was a truly amazing experience there behind the 2nd Maryland monument. It is something that we recommend you visit to see on your own. Maybe you, too, will have an experience like the one that CCPRS shared on that day.

The mass grave is surrounded by wooden logs and has confederate flags planted in the ground.

Chapter 2
Quick Haunts

Mark Sarro
The Lincoln Bedroom

In July of 2006, Kat and I were in town with members of CCPRS for the paranormal conference that was taking place at the Holiday Inn. Deciding to stay at the Farnsworth house, we booked the Lincoln room. It was a very nice room—a big four-post bed stood high off the ground and you needed a step to get up into the bed. The room had a Jacuzzi in the bathroom and it was very nice as well. In fact, it was all too nice. We really didn't need to stay in a room so special, considering how little we were going to be spending there with everything that we had going on that weekend with the conference and the other events that we were participating in.

The first night we stayed in the room there was the sense of something watching us. It seemed to be lurking about the room and stayed with us all night. We both had trouble sleeping because of the feeling that this *something* was in the room with us. It wasn't menacing or anything like that, but still, its presence could be felt and was unsettling. It was definitely there around us.

The Lincoln bedroom at the Farnsworth house where you have the feeling of being watched.

The second night was like the first; it seemed to be watching us and stayed in the room. I kept opening my eyes fully expecting to see a full apparition standing next to the bed, but that never happened. It simply made its presence known, but remained unseen. The second night I did sleep a little better; I was too tired to really care if a spirit was there or not.

Farnsworth House Inn
401 Baltimore Street
Gettysburg, PA 17325
www.farnsworthhouseinn.com

Carol Starr

CULP'S HILL—DARK FIGURE

On a beautiful evening in March, a friend and I decided to drive around the battlefield. We ended up on Culp's Hill. After walking around for awhile and enjoying the perfect evening, we got into the car and started to leave the area. We drove around the ranger's tower and just started to go down the hill, when something caught my eye.

I looked out of the car, and just off the road was a dark figure crouched down. It looked like it was facing in towards the woods. As I slowly drove by, it started to rise up. I saw a dark figure—it looked to be pretty tall—and its back was facing me.

Then, as I stopped briefly, I saw the figure slowly fade into nothing. Seeing this figure crouched down, looking out into the darkness, gave me a feeling of sadness. It seemed that he was still keeping a watch for the approaching enemy to this day.

A dark figure was kneeling, watching out towards the woods.

Carol Starr

EAST CAVALRY BATTLEFIELD

East Cavalry Battlefield is located three miles east of Gettysburg and was the place of heavy fighting between Union and Confederate Cavalry forces on July 3, 1863. The main fighting on the battlefield lasted for three hours. There is a privately-owned farm located there. This farm, owned by the Rummel family, was the site for much of the fighting during the dismounted phase.

To this day, as you drive along Low Dutch Road, you can still see the farm, which is still in the Rummel family. They also hold some secrets.

It is said that fourteen Confederate soldiers are buried somewhere along the lonely road. The family members are said to be the only ones who know the exact location of their graves and have kept that secret for generations.

So, if you're out one evening along that quiet stretch of road, you might be visited by a Confederate soldier still looking for the battle.

General Custer led his men to battle in these farmlands.

The battlefield where mounted soldiers fought.

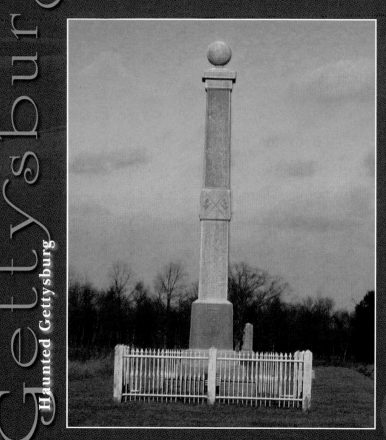

A monument on East Cavalry Battlefield.

Mark Sarro

HOLIDAY INN'S BATHROOM GHOSTS

During our weekend investigation of the Jennie Wade House and the Orphanage, CCPRS booked a group of rooms on the 5th floor of the Holiday Inn on Baltimore Street. CCPRS investigator Bob Meyer and I were sharing a room, and during the second night of our stay, we had a very brief, yet funny, experience in the room.

We were both lying in our beds and slowly beginning to fall asleep when there was a quick and sudden "SLAM!" coming from the bathroom. It was the toilet seat that had slammed shut. We jokingly made reference to a ghost and their bathroom habits and didn't think much of it.

Later, we found out that the group of

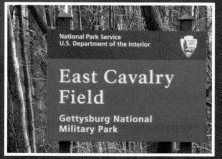

The sign at the entrance to East Cavalry battlefield.

rooms that we had all been staying in were considered to be actively haunted for the hotel and it was reported that often things would happen in the bathroom of one of the rooms.

The Holiday Inn was built on the site of a beautiful home that was occupied by relatives who lived in the Jennie Wade House. We spoke with a resident of Gettysburg who grew up in this house and were told that there was always paranormal activity, like footsteps and banging in the attic, which is now the top floor of the hotel.

The road going through East Cavalry battlefield where there are Confederate soldiers buried.

Chapter 3

The Jennie Wade House

Mark Sarro

A Brief History

The Jennie Wade House sits right along Baltimore Street. If you stand on the sidewalk on Baltimore Street facing the house you will see a statue of Jennie Wade herself. Jennie was born Mary Virginia Wade in 1843. Her friends and family would fondly call her Ginnie—short for Virginia, her middle name. It's believed that Jennie came about as the result of the misspelling of her name in a local paper.

The now-famous house that has come to be named after her never really was her home. The home itself is actually two homes, one side being the McClellan home and the other the McClain home.

Jennie and her family knew, that with the Civil War coming straight to their doorstep, they must

The front of the Jennie Wade house facing Baltimore Street.

take refuge somewhere safe. Jennie's older sister was about to have a baby and it was decided that it would be better for her to go stay at a friend's home—the McClellan home. She was joined by her younger brother, Jennie, and their mother.

Unfortunately for the Wade family, the house proved to be caught in the middle, right between the Confederate and Union soldiers. The house itself withstood 150 bullet holes and an artillery shell that came through the roof, through the wall, and lodged into a base board. Fortunately for the Wade family, the shell did not detonate. Otherwise it would have killed the whole family.

Her Daily Bread

Jennie had made it her custom to rise early and make bread to give to the passing Union soldiers. On this particular morning, July 3, 1863, it proved to be her last baking day. She was standing in the kitchen with an interior door open behind her when a stray bullet came through the exterior door, through the interior door, and entered Jennie at her left shoulder, fatally wounding her heart. She fell dead instantly.

Jennie's mother came rushing in and announced to her sister and brother that Jennie was dead. The screams and cries of the family at the loss of Jennie were heard from the street by passing Union soldiers. They rushed into the house to find Jennie laying dead on the floor and her family overtaken by grief. The soldiers quickly surmised how unsafe it truly was in the house and knew that they had to get the family to safety.

The cellar door was around the other side of the house on the McClain side. It was too dangerous to take the family outside and around to the cellar. The soldiers picked up Jennie's body and moved the family to the upstairs. The unexploded artillery shell had put a hole through the common wall between the two homes. The soldiers quickly began to break the hole out so that the family could pass into the other side and get down and into the cellar. After some frantic breaking and pounding, the soldiers managed make a hole big enough for everyone to pass through. They moved quickly through the hole and down the stairs. Just outside the door now was the access to the cellar.

The soldiers placed Jennie's body on some boards under a quilt in the basement. There the soldiers remained with the Wade family. Jennie's mother, brother, sister and new born niece remained in the basement through the day and into the night as the battle raged on outside. All the while they mourned the loss of the beloved Jennie.

Jennie's father, James, was not there with his family. At the time of Jennie's death, he had been residing in a local poor house, having been put there after he was convicted for minor offenses. He had originally been sent to Eastern State Penitentiary in Philadelphia, but the extreme isolation and solitude had caused him mental unrest. He was eventually released to and committed to a poor house that was local in Gettysburg.

It would be several years before James was told that his daughter had been killed. Even still; he would continue to ask how she was doing and where was she until his dying day.

A Flag of Honor

Jennie Wade was the only civilian to die in the battle of Gettysburg. She now rests in Evergreen Cemetery just a little farther up Baltimore Avenue, very near where Abraham Lincoln had given the famous "Gettysburg Address." There you will find her monument and the American flag raised above it. She is only one of two women in American history to have a flag over her grave; the other is Betsy Ross.

It was believed that the stray bullet may have in fact have come from a sniper that had been held up in the attic of the Farnsworth House not too far away.

Many visitors over the years have come to see the house and hear the story of Jennie and her family and how the events transpired that day; but hearing just the history wouldn't be all that a lot of visitors would experience. Many of these same visitors would come to have paranormal experiences while in the house. Some would see the spirits that remained there; others would hear them, and still more would feel them.

A very common experience shared by many who have come to visit and tour the house is that involving the chain that is hung across the room in front of the bed in a bedroom on the second floor of the McClain side of the house. The chain doesn't just sway back and forth, but it actually moves up and down. It moves and reacts as though someone was playing with it.

It is believed that there are several children spirits that come and visit the house. The orphanage is just across the street and it was thought that sometimes some of the children came and took refuge in the house.

One of the other spirits of the house is believed to be James, Jennie's father. It has been conjectured that he comes to the house out of remorse and regret that he did not get to see his daughter and be at her funeral after she died.

A Tour through the House

Over the past several years, CCPRS has come to visit the Jennie Wade House many times. Accompanied by several members of CCPRS at the time, I came to the house in May of 2006, visiting during a daytime tour. The tour guide began the tour on the McClellan

An artillery shell came through the room of the second-floor bedroom and crashed through this dividing wall. It never exploded. After, Jennie Wade's death, her body was carried up to this room and the wall was broken through to carry her to the other side and down to the basement.

side of the house, in the very room where Jennie had been shot and killed.

My first impression of the house was that it was small with relatively low ceilings; and I was amazed at its condition. It has been well cared for over the years and great concern has been given to keep it as close to how it was originally at the time that Jennie Wade and her family stayed there during the war.

The hard wood floors concealed no visitor—there was no mistaking if someone was in the house, because the floors creaked when you walked across them. Entering the house from the side door on the McClellan side, the bullet holes that had riddled the door and outside wall were visible. Upon entering, immediately to your left was the stairwell leading up to the second floor. The room was very square

with wallpaper that came down two thirds of the wall on all sides, with wood paneling then going to the floor. The wall on the right was where the entrance to the room that was used as a bedroom for Jennie's sister and where she'd had her baby. The interior door was left open and it too had the famous bullet hole from the bullet that came through the exterior door and then through this door, ultimately killing Jennie. In the corner, on the floor behind the door, is some of the original furniture that was in the house at the time that Jennie was killed. The floor boards where she had died had been replaced sometime after her death, but the original blood-stained boards remain in a private collection of a woman whose family once owned the house.

The stairs go up a few steps to a landing and then turn ninety degrees to go straight up to the second floor. There are two bedrooms joined to each other on the second floor. The ceilings are angled and follow the pitch of the roof. There is no attic in this house. The common wall that once separated the two homes now has an opening that allows access into the other home. This is where the artillery shell had come through the roof and through the wall and lodged itself in the base board on the McClain side of the house. There is a replica shell sticking out of the wall in the base board. The original shell is in the possession of the same woman who has the floor boards as mentioned earlier. The shell is still intact and never detonated.

The second floor of the McClain side of the house is very much like that of the McClellan side—two bedrooms joined together with an entry way with no door separating the two of them. The stairs going down to the first floor was on the same wall as the stairs on the McClellan side. Two conjoined rooms are on the first floor of the McClain side of the house as well. These rooms are set up as a sitting room and a parlor. The walls are adorned with photographs of the Wade family.

Out the side door; immediately to the left are the double cellar doors. The cellar covers both homes together. It appears that the wall between the two may have been opened up. There is an entrance at the other side of the cellar that no longer appears to be in use. The walls and floors are stone and there is a fireplace in the corner. The main room is now set up with rows of wooden benches. There is a display case on the same wall as the main entrance that has a painting depicting the time that the Wade family and soldiers held up in the basement during the battle. It was pointed out to me during a visit that the basement was in fact much smaller. The floors had been dug out and down extending the height of the basement another eighteen inches or more. The floor was originally a dirt floor. Along the back wall is the display where the mannequin of Jennie Wade lies under the quilt; representing where the actual body was placed during that time.

The house had made an impact on me. We sat there quietly in the basement at the end of our tour, and for a few moments, I thought about what it meant to have gone through the ordeal that the Wade family went through on that hot summer day, July 3rd, 1863.

Carol Starr

My First Visit to the Jennie Wade House

I was so excited to be spending the night in Gettysburg. This time, my family had spent a week up in Wellsboro, Pennsylvania, and on our way home, decided to spend the night in Gettysburg. It was October of 2000, and I was happy about seeing the town once again and going on my first ghost tour! After checking into the Quality Inn on Steinwehr Avenue, I saw a brochure about ghost tours of the Jennie Wade house.

I only had to wait a few minutes for the tour guide once we got to the historic Jennie Wade House. She appeared at the doorway appropriately dressed in a long black period dress with a black veil over her head and face. We started the tour behind the Jennie Wade House by a grouping of trees. While we were listening to her stories of ghostly soldiers wondering around the area, it started to rain, and after about fifteen minutes, it was coming down pretty good. The pouring rain gave it a very spooky feeling as I kept watch for anything that

The front entrance to the Jennie Wade House.

might appear out of the mist. We then continued with the tour inside the house.

Chained

This was my first visit inside the Jennie Wade House and it certainly didn't disappoint. We were taken from room to room and told of the many occurrences happening throughout the house, along with its rich history. As we gathered on the second floor in one of the bedrooms, I noticed the security chains start to move. I pointed it out to everyone else on the tour as well as the guide. What was unusual about the chains swinging was that it wasn't moving back and forth; it was swinging up and down as if there were small hands lifting them up and down.

As we all watched the chain moving in the one bedroom, it suddenly stopped. After a minute or two, the chain in the other bedroom started to do the same thing. We watched for a few minutes as the chains would alternate from room to room. No one was near the chains at any time.

I know I checked around for any hidden strings or anything else that could cause them to move. There wasn't anything that I could see. The guide, who said she was sensitive, said that she thought there was a little girl and a little boy that were playing with each other between the two bedrooms. You could almost see them romp through the rooms having a good time.

I believe that I enjoyed my visit to the Jennie Wade House as much as whoever was there that day playing within the two bedrooms. I also knew that I would be back.

Mark Sarro

INTERVIEW WITH JOE SVEHLA

Joe Svehla is the manager of Ghostly Images Tours and author of the Ghostly Images "Catch The Spirits" series. In November of 2007, it was arranged for Carol and me to formally meet Joe to conduct an interview for our book. We made arrangements to come and stay overnight in Gettysburg. Our expectations were unclear; we were hoping at best case scenario for an opportunity to spend a little time in the Jennie Wade House to conduct an EVP session and do a little bit of investigating. We had brought fellow investigators Kim and Kat with us on our trip.

We gathered at the Jennie Wade house museum and waited for Joe. Carol had already met Joe at a conference the previous July and had spent a good deal of time talking with him. Joe greeted us and then brought us over to the Jennie Wade house for a private tour. He began in the first floor on the McClellan side in the kitchen where Jennie had been shot and killed. Joe then began to tell us the history of Jennie and her family and how the events played out on that fateful day. Carol had her audio recorder going, camera, and

This is where Jennie Wade was the morning of July 3rd, making bread, when a bullet went through the door and struck her in the back, killing her instantly.

note of the environment for any strange or unusual occurrences. We moved into the bedroom where Jennie's sister had her baby. Carol had a very unusual experience at that time, which she didn't share until after we had left the house. She recounts the incident as follows:

"We went into the bedroom next to the kitchen area. This room was where Jennie's sister was resting after giving birth. As Joe was talking, I was taking pictures. I began to feel a light touch on my right ankle, as if a small hand was grabbing my ankle. My EMF meter was at 1.3. What was strange about this was that I was wearing jeans and the touch was under my jeans. I didn't say anything to anyone at that time."

Carol had the sensation of a child grabbing her ankle as she stood there and we listened to Joe. Later on, at another visit with Joe, Carol revealed her experience to Joe and he confirmed that, this had been reported by others as well. The children spirits that roamed the house were playful and often would reach out and grab a visitor to the house.

EMF meter in hand. She began taking pictures as Joe talked and told us the story.

A Child's Touch

I listened intently and had asked some questions as we went, trying my best at the same time to take

Mirror, Mirror

We continued our tour of the house and made our way upstairs to the second floor. Carol continued to take pictures and monitor her EMF meter. We had crossed over to the McClain side of the house and stood in the back bedroom that faced Baltimore Street. Joe continued to tell us stories as Carol took photos to document our visit. It was here that she captured a photo where it appears to show a faint outline of a woman wearing a long apron and bandana. We studied the photo intensely and on still another visit back to the house, made sure that Carol had not taken a picture of a photograph on the wall. It turned out to be a mirror hanging on the wall next to the window and not a photograph. She had in fact potentially caught the remnants of a spirit or apparition in her photograph.

A Tour is Born

We moved to the downstairs of the McClain side of the house and stood in the parlor. Joe explained to us the different photographs showing the Wade family on the wall. We then proceeded into the basement where he would finish his stories and talk about the various

A figure of a young boy has been spotted at the bottom of the stairs.

photographs in the collection of spirit photographs that had been assembled over the years. There must be literally hundreds of photographs that have been sent in by patrons who had visited and toured the house.

This was the birthplace of "Ghostly Images," the tour group that Joe began, as well as his series of books—a collection of the various stories told to him by visitors over the years.

We had completed our ghostly tour of the Jennie Wade house, but Joe had decided to take us over for a special tour of the Soldiers History Museum and the Orphanage. This story we will continue later…

Mark Sarro

A TALE OF GHOSTS PAST

Joe Svehla, told me this story while in the parlor of the Jennie Wade House during our formal investigation. One of the families who had come to live in the house some time after the Civil War would have a first-hand experience with the spirits.

It was late one evening and everyone had gone to bed. The family lived on the McClellan side of the house. They heard a loud commotion downstairs; in the room where Jennie had been shot and killed. The family rose and the children went to join their parents in the joining bedroom. They were all certain that there were intruders in the house.

They huddled together and listened as the sounds grew louder and the commotion continued on. Quickly, the sounds of terrible hustling and bustling made its way up the stairs towards the family. They were all certain now that they were about to come face to face with their intruders; but as the sounds grew louder and nearer, no one came into appearance. The sounds and commotions came straight towards them and then turned and went through the wall, down the stairs, and out through the other house right in front of them. The family could hardly believe what had just happened.

It seems that the events of the soldiers coming into the house and finding Jennie dead on the floor had played itself out all over again. Was this a residual energy of those traumatic events? Did the family witness the replay of the events firsthand as they would have happened at the time of the horrible event? It's an amazing story and rare one at that—for that experience has not been reported by anyone else other then family who lived in the house at that time.

CCPRS Formal Investigation February 15, 2008

We were given the opportunity to come and formally investigate the Jennie Wade house in February of 2008. This was an opportunity that Carol and myself had been hoping for ever since either one of us ever stepped foot into the house. We knew that the house had to be active, and to have a chance to privately study and investigate it would be the best possible opportunity that we could have hoped for.

This investigation was the first one of our weekend. It had also been arranged for us to investigate the Soldiers History Museum on the following night. Our team consisted of Carol, Kim, Kat, Isaac, Bob, Melissa,

Ken and me. Joe and his wife, Karen, would join us and a fellow tour guide, Bob Michaels, would also be joining us later in the evening.

The investigation was set to begin at 6pm. It was decided that we would make the parlor on the first floor of the McClain side of the house our base of operations. This is where we would put all of our equipment and set up the DVR system for monitoring the various cameras placed throughout the house. Bob and I quickly got to work setting up the cameras; we had decided to point a camera facing towards the bottom of the stairs from the parlor. It had been reported that a full-body apparition had been seen at the landing on the stairwell, and for that reason, having a camera there made good sense.

We also placed a camera in the basement facing towards the wall where the display with the mannequin was setup. Another camera was placed on the second floor of the McClain side in the front bedroom facing towards the back. Several camcorders on tripods were situated in various places of the house as well.

Tonight was going to be a special night; this would only be the second investigation that the ITC Device Prototype II would be used, and for many in the group, this would be their first time participating in an ITC session. Bob, Melissa, and I had all used it together on a private investigation not too far away from Gettysburg the previous month. We all knew that it was something special due to the surprising amount of EVPs collected during that investigation.

What is ITC?

Okay, let's now take a step aside to talk about what ITC and the ITC device actually is. ITC stands for Instrumental Trans Communication. ITC is the parent of EVP, video feedback, talking boards, pendulums, etc. Essentially, it's communication with the spirit realm by means of a device; in our case the ITC Device Prototype II, a device that I built based off of the inspiration of Bob's device ITC Device Prototype I.

ITC research started many years before with numerous investigators and researchers throughout the field; it begins with Thomas Edison. He believed that a device with which one could have direct communication with the other side would be man's single greatest invention. It was recently discovered that there had been many pages written on the subject in his memoir which General Electric had originally omitted; but just recently, these pages have come to light.

The ITC Device Prototype I and II are within the same family of devices as the "Frank's Box."

Frank Sumption is the inventor of the "Frank's Box," a device created from various ham radio parts that works by providing a continuous sweep through the radio frequencies, creating a linear sweep. The basic principle is that by creating this sweep through the frequencies, you can create a RF (Radio Frequency) field that will facilitate communication with the spirit realm. A sweep is basically moving through the radio stations quickly.

How these devices vary from traditional EVP recordings is that when you conduct a standard EVP session using a digital or analog audio recorder, you ask questions aloud while recording and usually you would not "hear" any answers to your questions until playback. For most investigators, this would be post investigation. The "Frank's Box," ITC Device, etc., is much different. When you ask a question, if there is someone there to communicate, you will hear the answer in real time!

The implications of such a device have dramatically affected the way that an investigation and EVP/ITC sessions are conducted, because by hearing the response to a question in real time, you can immediately change the direction and line of questioning and be more specific to the answers that you are receiving. In a standard EVP session, you ask the questions and really don't know if you will get an answer or if you are even asking the right questions. This has always been a

challenge, and for me personally, was something that at times could be frustrating because you didn't really know if you were in fact communicating with someone.

Our first formal investigation with ITC Device Prototype II was amazing because of the amount of EVPs that we recorded and documented. We conducted three sessions that had varied in length from about twenty-five to forty minutes per session. We were astonished when during our evidence analysis we would come to find that between the Device and standard EVPs recordings, we had captured nearly 60 EVPs! To that date, I had never come close to capturing even half as many EVPs. During some of our more notable investigations (Fort Mifflin and Eastern State Penitentiary), we had maybe come away with ten or more EVPs, but certainly not sixty!

I'd also like to take a moment to tell you about the different types of EVPs. EVPs can basically be separated into three classes; A, B, and C. A *Class A* EVP is one where you clearly hear and understand what is being said, whether it's a single word or phrase. A *Class B* EVP is one where the voice is not as clearly audible and the interpretation to what is being said can be left to debate, but it is certain that it is a voice, male, female, or child, and that something is clearly being said. A *Class C* EVP is where the more mechanical and whispery type of EVPs reside. These voices are there and what is being said isn't very clear at all. It is understood that there is a voice and a definite break in the pattern of the audio signal, but what is being said is uncertain. The interpretation of what the word or phrase is saying is left to the listener.

Now let's apply these classes to how they are heard within the ITC Device itself. On our particular devices, during the linear sweep of the radio frequency band (AM Frequency), you will hear a clicking sound as the frequencies pass. Some participants in our sessions have complained about the clicking sound and that can be an inherent drawback to utilizing the specific radios that we used for our devices, but I found it useful as a way to gauge the potential authenticity of the EVP. If the word or phrase that was being said spanned several clicks or more, than that was further proof that it could not be a random coincidence or background radio chatter. When a voice comes through on the device, it will sit on top of the signal of the linear sweep and in a *Class A* EVP, it is quite clear and obvious that it is not a random clip from a passing radio frequency or station. *Class B* and *Class C* EVPs on these devices can be a little more tricky to pull out, but again, they follow the same pattern of sitting on top of the signal and will span several frequencies or clicks of the linear sweep.

ITC in Gettysburg

My device is setup to use with a laptop computer or it can be used as a standalone, but I prefer to have the laptop used with it. The output of the audio can be recorded directly into the laptop and an audio frequency analysis can be performed at the same time. Participants who use the device will have headphones on so that they can better hear the device and any possible voices that may come through.

At the time that the device was used during the Jennie Wade House investigation, a podium condenser microphone was used to record the questions being asked of the device and to pick up the ambient sounds of the room.

Carol and I have written about the investigation in a way to include the exact transcripts from the ITC sessions during the investigation. This way, you will be able to see just how the investigators reacted and interacted with the device.

There is much debate and controversy over these devices; one debate is the inherent danger of opening up a "portal" to which you are inviting something to come through. The argument has been made to not even use these devices in reportedly haunted locations because of the potential of this danger. We have taken this debate/argument seriously and realize that there is the potential for danger when using a device like this.

We have had experiences on numerous occasions where something that we were communicating with started cursing at us! This is even further proof that it could not in fact be random radio chatter coming through the device and being misinterpreted as spirit phenomenon. We realized quickly the importance of setting up guidelines and parameters when conducting these sessions; taking care not open up and invite something that does not belong there. These devices are proving that they not only facilitate communication with spirits that may be residing in a particular location, but also seems to be a beacon for any spirit that may wish to communicate.

Now it was time to split up into two teams and begin the formal investigation. Very early on we immediately began to have equipment problems in the basement. The DVR camera would not work properly upon setting it up and proved to be problematic throughout the course of the night. My team consisted of Ken, Kat, and Kim and Carol's team was made up of Bob, Melissa, Isaac, and herself. My team was going to conduct an ITC Session on the second floor in the main bedroom on the McClellan side of the house and Carol's team was going to conduct and ITC session in the basement using Bob's ITC Device Prototype I.

Mark Sarro

The McClellan Side Second-Floor Bedroom

It was time to start our formal investigation. My team consisted of Kat, Ken, Kim and myself (from CCPRS). We also had Joe and Karen with us and Bob Michaels joined us mid-session (from Ghostly Images Tours and our hosts). I had set up my ITC Device Prototype II in the second floor bedroom that faces Baltimore Street; this was also in the front home of the two conjoined homes that made up the Jennie Wade House (The McClellan side).

It was a clear and brisk night that mid-February with very few clouds in the sky; this is important because of the strange occurrence that we would have only a few minutes into the session. Joe had his set of copper dowsing rods that he liked to use during EVP sessions; he said that he felt fairly successful with them and I too was curious to see how they would interact with my team and the environment in the house.

We gathered around on the floor as I started the ITC device. We all had headphones on so we could better hear what the device might say. I had asked Kat

35

to lead the session in asking the questions for the group. Ken was monitoring EMF and Temperature readings, Kim was doing video documentation, and I was running and monitoring the ITC device and audio recording. Joe sat back against the wall on the ledge to the left of the doorway that connected the two homes. Karen was sitting closer within the group. The ITC device was running; clicking and clacking as it swept through the AM frequency bands on the modified radio. I was monitoring frequency response and the recording software as the device ran.

I noticed that I was hearing a strange sound coming through over the microphone. It sounded like rain hitting the window panes of the window directly behind me in the corner. I took my headphones off and looked around and asked, "Is it raining?"

"I don't think so," Kim replied.

"It sounds like rain hitting the window; does anyone else hear that?" I remarked and asked again.

"No, I don't think that it is, but yes I hear it, too," Kat replied.

The interesting thing is that we did in fact catch the event on video; and you can clearly hear in the video that it sounds as though rain is hitting against the windows. It in fact was not raining, and as I had mentioned earlier, it was a cold, but clear night. We

The chains move back and forth and up and down in this bedroom. You can almost see children running back and forth playing.

then turned our attentions back towards the session as Kat asked her first question.

Questions for the Other Side

"Is there anyone here who would like to introduce themselves to us?" Kat asks aloud to the room. The room goes silent as we all wait and listen for a response. The radio sweep continues… click, click, click…

"Please come tell us your name?" Kat asks inquisitively. "We'd really like to talk to you."

She tries again. "Is there something you would like to tell us?"

Silence remains in the room. I look to monitor what everyone is doing. Ken is busy overseeing the EMF and temperature gauges as he writes notes in his book. Kim scans the room with the camera as she turns her focus back to Kat. Joe and Karen listen quietly as this is their first ITC session using a device like the one that I brought to the investigation. I turn my attentions back to the device and await Kat's next question.

"Are there any children here with us?" Kat asks aloud as she looks around the room. "How do you feel about us being in your house?"

The device is running and we have yet to hear the definitive answer to our question that we had been so intensely listening for.

"How long have you lived here in this house?"

Silence still holds true; Ken shuffles on the floor and I am still remarking to myself how at times I can still hear the sounds of the rain hitting the window.

"I feel kind of silly; I don't remember what the date is today, what's the date today?" She asks forgetfully.

One of the approaches that we've adopted with our EVP and ITC sessions was to try and have simple conversation, to almost lure the spirits out with questions in a way that would explain why we would be even asking these kinds of questions.

I have always had trouble with asking the standard interrogative line of questioning and doing it in such a way that would come across very cold and impersonal. I looked at it simply from a conversational stand point; I don't believe that if I were an intelligent spirit that I would be so inclined to answer questions that were asked in the typical fashion.

I have also found that at times EVPs can be caught when there is other conversation going on and not always during a formal EVP session where questions are being asked.

"How many people live in this house? What are the kid's names? What kind of games do you like to play?" Kat makes her queries with pauses of about thirty seconds or more between each question.

At this point during the session, the ITC device goes dead and the session temporarily stops. I could not determine the cause of the disruption, but notated it in our logs and reports. We started the session again just a few moments later and Kat began asking questions again.

"Were you playing with the lights downstairs earlier?" she asks.

The lights in the parlor on the first floor had reacted strangely. This is where we had set up our base with the DVR system.

"Does anyone hear knocking at the door?" Kat asks aloud to the group. We all paused and looked at each other; we had heard some knocking but were not sure as to where these sounds had originated.

"Please come in here and talk to us; we'd like to talk to you…" she remarks. "Please introduce yourself, my name is Katharine."

An inaudible male voice comes through on the device; it was captured on the recording, but what it said was unclear.

Kat, feeling encouraged that she was getting a response, asks the question, "What's your name? Are you scared of us? We're not here to hurt you; we want to help you… Please help us to help you."

Knocking sounds are heard again coming from another part of the house. Ken writes it into his notes as Kim scans the room again with the video camera in the hopes of capturing something.

"How do you feel about these cold winters in Gettysburg? Do you use wood stoves or coal stoves here? You use wood, don't you? Is it hard to keep this house heated and warm?" Kat has a certain sensitivity where she is able to pick up a response like an imprint. Sometimes they come to her audibly or visually, and when she is not ready for them, it can take her by surprise.

"How much do you love this house? Did you grow up in this house? What do you know about this house?"

More knocking sounds are heard coming from the other room. It is important to note that the other team is downstairs in the basement in the other home and not in this house at all.

"What do you know about this house that we might not know? Or maybe someone here *does* know? What are the kid's names?"

A knocking sound is heard again; we notate it, but keep quiet hoping that we will hear a direct answer to Kat's questions on the ITC device.

"Where do you like to walk in this house?"

Knocking sounds are heard again; somewhere nearby, yet in another part of the house.

"What are your favorite rooms?" she asks. "My mother always said that the heart of the home was in the kitchen. Is that your favorite place to be?" She makes a statement followed up with a question.

More knocking sounds are heard. It seems that it is responding by making a noise rather than communicating directly with us via the ITC device.

"Are these the children's rooms up here? Do the children have any favorite toys? Do you have any questions for us? Is there anything that you would like to tell us?"

The knocking sounds almost like walking or pacing about and is clearly heard on the audio recording from the session. An unknown voice then comes through on the device, but again what it says is inaudible and none of us are able to quite make it out the message.

"Is there someone that you miss? Why do you keep pacing? What's wrong? Why are you pacing?" she asks again.

I notice that the knocking sound is consistent, but still cannot determine where in the house it is coming from.

"Is there something that you would like to say to Joe?" she asks.

More knocking sounds are heard... I lean over to Ken and ask him to be sure to notate the time, temperature, and EMF readings when we hear the knocking sounds.

"Where do the children like to play in the house?" She pauses. "What's that?" Kat asks as though she hears a direct response, but none of us hear it.

At this point, I announce how far along we are into the session. As mentioned before, we typically try to keep EVP and ITC sessions to a half hour/forty-five minutes at most, at any given time.

Heavy footsteps are heard coming up the stairs behind us from the other home and Bob Michaels enters the room. Unfortunately, he wasn't quite expected and startled Kat. We ended the first session and decided to chat for a few moments before continuing.

A very interesting thing started to happen. Joe had been using his dowsing rods during the session to make communication in his own way. The rods had started spinning and Kim was kneeling down on the floor on one knee, beneath him. I remarked to Kim, "The rods are spinning right above your head."

Kim looks up very cautiously and asks, "Were they spinning before I sat down?"

Joe replies, "No, they were not!"

Were spirits trying to communicate with Joe while he was using his dowsing rods? I decided to turn the session over to Joe. His history with the house was important. He had spent many hours working in the home and had had several very interesting experiences over the years of his own. Participating in numerous investigations, he had been hosting paranormal groups for several years. I decided to keep the ITC device running, but our focus has now turned to Joe and his use of the dowsing rods.

He intended to use them as a way of communicating directly with the spirits of the house. The idea is simple; if the rods crossed, then it was responding with a "yes" to a direct question, or some believe that when simply "dowsing" in an environment, that when they cross, that is a sign of a spirit presence. I can't say that I have a formal opinion one way or the other. I too at one point invested in a pair of copper dowsing rods for research purposes, but had not used them on many formal investigations. I had observed others from varied groups on more than one occasion and I will have to say that, at times, they have yielded some very interesting results.

Joe starts out with his first question. "Did you live in the house?" he asks. The rods remain still, not responding to his question.

"Were you related to the first family that lived here?" The left rod turns inward, indicating "no" as an answer to his question.

"Were you living here in the 1890's?"

"No," the rods answer.

"Are you a child here?"

"Yes." The rods answer as they cross in the middle.

"Are you a little boy?"

"No."

"Are you a little girl?"

"Yes."

"Do you like when people come to visit the house?" The rods hold steady without a response.

"Do you like it when children come to the house?" Joe asks.

"Do you want to play with those toys?" Kat asks aloud. The rods slowly cross to answer "Yes."

"Should we have brought a dolly? Maybe next time we will bring a dolly..." she says.

"Do you have long hair?" Kat asks, and the rods slowly say, "Yes."

"Are you alone in the house?" Joe asks.

The rods swing to a resounding "No."

"Are there other children in the house?" He asks.

The rods say, "No."

"Did you ever live in the orphanage?" Kat asks.

The rods do not respond.

"Are you happy here in the house?" Joe asks.

The rods cross to answer, "Yes."

"You felt safe here in this house?" Kat asks.

The rods answer, "Yes."

"Who took care of you here?" Kat asks.

The rods do not respond.

Joe has a connection to the house; all the time that he had spent there and the numerous EVP and dowsing rod sessions that he participated in have provided him with answers over time. He believes he knows who some of the spirits are that come to the house and you will read with his next few questions as he begins to hone into exactly who it is that is there visiting with us.

"Are your mother and father here with you?" he asks.

The rods swing to answer, "No."

"Is your mother here with you?"

Again, the rods swing to answer, "No".

"When you came here, were you ten years old when you lived in the house?"

The rods answer, "Yes." Joe now had everyone's direct attention. We sat silently observing as he continued to ask his questions to the spirit.

"Does Jennie Wade ever come to visit the house?"

The rods do not answer.

"Does Harry Wade ever come visit the house?"

The rods continue to remain still. We watch and wait...

"Is there a boy named Willy who comes to the house?"

The rods do not answer. I begin to think that whoever it was there visiting with us, that we had lost the connection with them and that they had moved on.

"Are there any soldiers in the house?"

The rods answer, "No."

"Do you feel safe in the house?"

The rods again answer, "No."

Joe has a curious look on his face as we all look at each other in reaction to the rods. I wonder to myself, "What is this girl afraid of?"

It was worth noting too that earlier the rods told a different story, but we find that when using this method, you might get answers that contradict earlier statements or answers to questions because there could be different spirits trying to communicate to you.

"Why don't you feel safe in the house? Is there someone in the house that you are afraid of?"

The rods swing to a resounding, "Yes."

"Okay, is this person a man?"

The rods swing and answer, "Yes."

"Where in the house is he? Is he here in the room with you?"

The rods answer, "No."

"Is he downstairs in the bedroom?"

The rods answer, "No."

"Is he in the basement?"

The rods again answer with a strong, "Yes."
Here I have to interject an interesting note.

Strange But True

This entire session happened in less than an hour. CCPRS typically will keep its investigative rotations to forty-five minutes to an hour tops. The contributing factors are based on how much activity there is, how big the location we are investigating is, and in how many different places activity has been reported.

Keep in mind now, that while all of this is going on, Carol's investigative team is in the basement. Their first session ended in catastrophic equipment failure. They, too, had intended on having an ITC session, but the device failed on all counts and would not turn on, make any sounds, or work in any way. We generally change our batteries in any piece of equipment that we will use on an investigation at the beginning of the night. It's a precaution to help prevent equipment failure and ensure that the equipment will work throughout the night.

With that said, it is very common that electronic devices fail and cease working when paranormal activity may be present. One of the running theories in the field is that batteries will drain from devices

as the paranormal activity begins to manifest. I personally have experienced this type of phenomena on numerous investigations, and to know that this was what was going on at the same time that we had a little girl telling us through Joe and his dowsing rods that there was someone in the basement that she was afraid of was incredibly eye-opening.

Very shortly after the girl communicated to us that she was afraid of someone in the basement the communication stopped and we ended the session. I then turned to stop the ITC device and recorder and we proceeded to go downstairs to the parlor. This is where I came to find Bob and talked to him about what had happened in the basement. I found it to be very strange, but was interested to see if anything else would happen. I had convinced Bob that they should try again and this time that they could use *my* ITC device.

It wouldn't be until sometime later in the weeks that followed the investigation that the events that took place during that first ITC session happened the way that they did; to know that while we were deep in communication with the child on the second floor who was afraid of the "man" in the basement that Carol and her team was having catastrophic equipment failure at the same time. I can't help but think that we were caught up in a power struggle between the spirit of the overbearing man in the basement and the timid child that was communicating with us via ITC and dowsing rods on the second floor.

It would be a few months later when we would return to present our findings to Joe and Bob that we would hear the EVP that was caught in the basement just the week before our investigation. The recording goes on for nearly three minutes of what sounds like dialogue between a man with a deep gruff voice and a child who at times sounds like she is humming! Since then, Bob and I have played this particular EVP on our radio show "Voices Carry" and it has caused quite a controversy among our audience. The show is in our archives on www.voicescarryradio.com/showarchive.htm.

Carol Starr
THE BASEMENT

We started our session approximately at 9:15pm. We had an EMF base reading of .1 to .3 and our base temperature reading was 50.7 degrees.

Bob began the session with a testing of the audio levels and hitting the record button. We then all introduced ourselves. One of the important things when doing any kind of EVP work is to speak in your natural voice. If you whisper, you could mistake your voice for an EVP and that might hurt your evidence. So, we started by saying our names and giving the time.

Questions for the Other Side

Melissa asked the first question. "Is there anybody here with us that would like to say Hello?"

Bob then announces that he's changing the band on the frequency.

Melissa asks, "Hello, can you hear me on that?" You can hear street noise from outside.

Bob asks, "Are there any spirits or entities that are here with us tonight? Would you like to speak with us?" (As a group and as mentioned earlier, we generally leave approximately twenty to thirty seconds between questions.)

Melissa then says, "My name is Melissa, what's your name?"

We hear **"MARY"** from the ITC device.

Because we knew that when using the ITC device, we would hear answers to our questions in real time, we could tailor our questions accordingly.

Melissa asks, "Can you speak up? We can't quite hear you; speak louder for us. What is your name?" We hear boards creaking.

Melissa asks, "How old are you?"

Bob asks, "Is there a male presence down here in the basement that would like to communicate with us?" We hear more boards creaking.

After being killed, Jennie's body was taken here until the battle was over. Does she still roam the darkened cold basement?

Bob asks, "Are there any Confederate or Union soldiers that would like to speak with us tonight?"

We hear **"MICHELLE"** from the ITC device.

Bob asks, "Can you tell us Michelle who? Give us a last name or a surname please."

Melissa asks, "Is there a female presence down here that would like to speak with us?"

"NO" (male voice).

Bob asks, "Is Jennie Wade's father here with us tonight in the basement?" We hear boards creaking once again.

Melissa says, "I hear banging and rapping."

Bob asks, "Come again; is that you? Is that Jennie Wade's father?"

Melissa asks "How do you feel about General Lee?" Pause. "Say that again?"

Bob says, "That was me putting the meter down..." (You can hear camera noise.)

Melissa says, "I think I heard *precious* twice."

Bob says, "That outside?"

Melissa asks, "Jennie Wade, are you here with us tonight?"

"Who is president?" (You can hear Bob's jacket rustling.)

Bob asks, "Carol, do you want to say anything? Do you want to ask some questions?"

I ask, "Is there anyone here that has a message for us?"

Bob says, "There are footsteps walking upstairs."

I ask, "Do you like us here tonight or do you want us to leave?"

Melissa asks "Are you afraid of anyone here with us in the room?"

We hear **"YES."**

Melissa asks, "Are you afraid of anyone here with us in the room?" Melissa says to us, "I keep hearing *precious* over and over again."

Bob says, "I'm not getting anything."

Melissa asks, "Who are you afraid of?"

We hear, **"PRECIOUS."**

Bob asks, "Are you guys hearing it?"

As you can tell, by this point, we are all getting excited because we keep hearing the word *precious* coming from the ITC device. After a couple of minutes, we all decide that it is a "loop" that we are hearing. When the device hit a certain frequency, it kept repeating itself. A few minutes of excitement, but we figured it out and continued on with our session.

While we were checking out the ITC device, Bob says, "Couple of minutes, let's see if we hear it again."

After he says that, I got an EVP on my audio recorder. It sounds like a whisper, and it's a male voice saying "emmmm or end."

I ask, "Were you ever at Eastern State Penn?"

"YES," a voice from the ITC device says.

Bob says, "That could have been her father."

(This was a fact that was told to us by Joe Svehla from Ghostly Images, and we had also done some research regarding it. Jennie's father did serve time there.)

I ask, "Was your name James?"

We hear **"AHA"** from the ITC device.

I ask, "James, why are you here? Are you here because of Jennie?"

Melissa asks, "Why were you in Eastern State Penn?"

I ask, "James, what do you do for a living?"

Melissa asks, "How old are you? Do you have any children?"

I ask, "Do you like the children that are here in this house?"

Melissa asks, "Can you make the chain move for us?" (There is a chain that goes from one end of the wall to the other between the benches and the "body" of Jennie Wade.)

Melissa asks, "Are you bored with us?"
We hear *"YES"* from the ITC device.
Melissa asks, "Would you like us to leave?"
I ask, "Would you like us to stay?"
Bob says, "Let's cut it off here."

We didn't experience any fluctuation in temperature or EMF during our session in the basement and this session in the basement ended at 9:45pm.

Strange But True

I have to say that the session in the Jennie Wade House basement left me with many questions regarding who is haunting the basement and why. Is it Jennie's father who is still looking for his daughter after he was never told of her sudden death? Or could the spirits be some of the soldiers who were fighting each other on either side of the house? I feel that there is something in the basement that is trying to communicate with the living when they visit The Jennie Wade House.

Carol Starr

THE FIRST-FLOOR BEDROOM

After our break, we headed to the first-floor bedroom located right next to the kitchen. Jennie was in the kitchen on July 3, 1863, kneading bread when the bullet came through the outside door and an inner door to killed her instantly.

Our session began at 10:10pm.
Melissa asks, "Is there anybody here with us that would like to communicate with us? What is your name? Do you live here? Do you like to bake here?"
I ask, "Was there a baby born in this room?"
Melissa asks, Are there any children here with us that would like to play? Is there a James with us?"
Bob asks, Are there any Confederate or Union astral beings that are dwelling here in this presence? Can you tell us who is winning the war? Do you know General Lee? Do you know that the Confederate army surrendered at Appomattox Court?"
Melissa asks, "Can I say something?" She pauses and turns to look at me, saying, "Just came to me:

That'll never happen." This was a phrase that she'd heard in her own mind as though projected there by an outside source. She said again, "The answer came to me."

Bob asks, "Can you tell us who George Pickett is? Who is General Grant? Do you like President Abraham Lincoln? Do you like him?"

Melissa asks, "Can you sing a marching song for us?"

Bob asks, "What regiment in the army are you from? Old Virginia?"

Melissa asks, "Can you sing a marching song for us?"

I ask, "Are there any Southern Gentlemen here tonight?" The noise of a camera is heard as someone snaps a picture. "Does anyone know what happened in the next room?"

"YES"

Bob asks, "Who Shot Jennie Wade?"

"ME"

Melissa says, "I heard 'ME' loud and clear." She pauses. "Who is ME? Tell us your name."

****Possible EVP**** *Breathing*

"I'm sorry I didn't introduce myself…I'm Melissa. What is your name?"

I ask, "Do you feel bad that you shot her?"

"5" or "FIRE"

Carol says, "Did you fire the fatal shot?"

"YES"

Melissa asks, "Was it an accident or did you do it on purpose?"

I ask "If you knew you shot her, did you help carry her down into the basement?"

"YES"

Bob asks, "Who gave you orders to shoot at this house?"

"THE BLACK"

Melissa asks, "Can you repeat that please for us?"

I ask, "Were you down the street at the Farnsworth House when you fired the gun?"

Melissa asks, "Are you a sharp shooter?"

Bob asks, "What year is it? Do you know what year it is?"

Melissa asks, "Who do you follow?"

"CONFEDERATE" *A female voice says on the device.*

Bob says, "I thought it said seven, but a female voice."

Melissa asks, "Do you fight for the Confederate side? Do you feed Confederates?"

Bob says to us, "That was Melissa's tape that snapped." Then, "Can you make something in here move for us? Can you show us any sign of your presence here? Make a noise, move something, a curtain or a bed sheet."

Melissa asks, "Can you jump up and down on the floor?"

"MY WINDOW" The device calls out in a mechanical voice.

Bob says, "It is moving a bit over there." He motions as he refers to the curtain on the window. We went over to the window to check for drafts and found none.

Melissa asks, "Are you by the window?"

"HELP" The device says.

Bob says, "I don't know if…"

Melissa says, "We're going to check this window out."

I say, "Go ahead and touch him, he's over here by your window."

"I'M COLD" The device replies.

Melissa asks, "Can you make Bob feel cold too?"

"DON'T KNOW HOW" The device then says.

Carol says, "Can you touch Bob?" Then, "Is it drafty."

Bob says, "No"

Melissa asks, "Can you move the other curtain over here for us? Come stand in front of this window. Did you move something in the other room? What?"

"SAVING UP" The device says.

I ask, "Is your picture hanging in this room?"

We received quite a few answers to our questions from the ITC device and also had an EVP. Bob also comments in his report by saying:

"Personally, the investigation of The Jennie Wade House in Gettysburg was of great interest to me. I was honored as an investigator to be given the opportunity to investigate such a great location… As an investigator/tech specialist for CCPRS, the Jennie Wade House was a bit of a challenge for our tech department. The house is tight and small (stairways) in places and the house winds throughout. Due to the house's age, the floors creaked often and the house was not well insulated. This made evidence gathering challenging to the team and members of the group often heard footsteps, loud noises, and creaking throughout the house. Cold spots were also felt and this was mainly attributed to the openness and age of the home.

Though these obstacles were challenging to the team, this did not take away from the excitement of investigating the location. After a general walk through of the residence, our team decided to go with a four camera DVR setup as the main source of video in the investigation. We decided to run two cameras upstairs on the second floor, another in the kitchen where Jennie Wade was shot and killed, and finally a camera in the basement. We also ran a Digital 8 camcorder during an ITC session upstairs on the second floor. A mini DV camcorder was used during a lights out vigil to close out the evening investigation...

In conclusion, I can honestly conclude from the evidence CCPRS has gathered and the experiences that members had while investigating the location, it would be my recommendation to label The Jennie Wade House as a paranormally active site."

Carol Starr

SECOND-FLOOR BEDROOM

After a short break, we then went to investigate the upper floor where there are two bedrooms on either side of the house.

As we were walking through the one bedroom, I noticed a mirror hanging on the wall. I had taken a photograph of that mirror on our last visit to the house back on November 10, 2007. In that picture there was a figure with a white kerchief and long skirt/apron. I wanted to confirm that it was indeed a mirror and not a painting or picture. I kept seeing the photo over and over in my mind, knowing that somehow I must have been mistaken—it had to be a trick of light, some likeness reflected of a painting. But no, here was the evidence before me yet again. I was not mistaken. There had indeed been a face in that mirror. But whose? Would I ever find out? I put it out of my head for the moment. Time would tell—or not.

We proceeded into the next room to sit quietly and record. I experienced a cold spot that ran up my back, making me shiver. I was standing at the foot of the bed and next to the sloped ceiling. The coldness went through me very fast and when I turned around, I was able to track it back to the corner of the room.

Melissa came over with an EMF meter and tracked it back in the corner, then along the back of the wall. As we were exiting the upper bedroom, I noticed a dress that I had seen before with two books lying on top of each other. When I saw them earlier, they were at either end of the dresser. I asked the other investigators to see if they had moved them and no one. Who had moved these items, I wondered. Was it just our imaginations or was something of a paranormal nature going on here? It was common for me to hear that things in a haunted location moved from one place to another—and then sometimes back to their original spots. This then, was just another thing that put us on edge.

This second-floor bedroom is very small and has a sloped roof. This is where an artillery shell blasted through the roof and also through the brick dividing wall and into the bedroom on the opposite side of the house. This room was where Jennie Wade's family along with Union soldiers brought her body after she had been killed. It wasn't safe to bring her out of the house through the kitchen area, so they carried her upstairs, laid her down in this room until they had made the hole bigger in the brick wall, then carried her through and downstairs to the basement.

Personally, I can't imagine hearing cannon fire, gun shots, shouts, and the battle going on all around you, while trying to carry a member of your family up through the house, and then have to chop your way through a brick wall to crawl through and carry her down to the dark basement. A family (including a newborn) huddled together in grief and terror, waiting until the battle finally is over...

The following is from our investigation in that bedroom that started around 10:45pm. We first made our introductions.

Bob says, "Did you feel cold? A Cold Spot."

Melissa says, "Yeah."

I reply, "I didn't feel anything over here, something back there, a cold feeling."

Sounds of walking on the floor (us) cough (us)

I say, "Ohhhh; cold, cold right over here, right behind me. It's cold."

Isaac says, "Take a picture."

I say, "That's the first I felt that, maybe walk through, I had a feeling when I first came up here, low ceiling. EMF .7 .8 and a dark shadow; right up my back."

Bob says, "There's no..."

Melissa says, "There's something over here in his corner because when we move away it drops right down."

Bob says, "What are some of the readings?"

Melissa says, "1.1 right now."

I say, "I kept sensing something behind me."

Melissa says, ".7 EMF back there."

Bob says, "Some old wires."

I say, "This roof must be exposed; that shell came from right here, never exploded."

Melissa says, "Do objects carry EMF?"

I say, "Yes."

Melissa says, "I got a .7" "moving into another room."

I say, "Talking about photograph (mirror), temp 75 to 81 degrees in earlier base reading by that mirror. Book on stand was on top of other book."

As I was exiting the bedroom, I happened to glance over to the dresser by the door. I felt something was wrong, and as I approached the dresser, I realized that the books that had been sitting on the top had been moved. I looked around and no one was nearby. At the beginning of the evening on our initial tour, the two books had been lying separate on the top of the dresser, now, they were stacked on top of each other. Was this the work of a spirit that likes to tidy up their room?

Carol Starr

A Review of the Evidence

The investigation proved to be filled with personal experiences had by several investigators during the course of the evening. We had gathered quite a bit of footage to review from the investigation; in total there was over thirty hours of video footage, over ten hours of audio recordings, and hundreds of photographs to be reviewed.

It can take quite some time to properly review the materials and to pull out any potential positive evidence collected. We take great care in the way that we gather our evidence and then review it. The normal ratio we've found is that for every hour of audio or video footage captured, it will take about two hours to properly review and document. We knew, based off of the experiences during the ITC sessions, that in fact we did have some EVP evidence, but we were not expecting as many traditional EVPs to be captured on the various digital and analog recorders that we used. We were also very pleased to find that we had also captured some video evidence of possible paranormal activity as well.

Seein' is Believin'

Video Transcripts

As mentioned, we had a four camera DVR system setup throughout the house along with several additional stationary camcorders that had been set upon tripods in different parts of the house. There was a camera pointing from the parlor on the McClain side of the house towards the stairs, a camera in the basement facing towards the wall where the mannequin lays beneath the quilt in the corner representing Jennie Wade's body, a camera on the second floor of the McClain side of the house pointed from the front bedroom towards the back where the stairway is. The camera's focus point was the chain that had segmented off the room from the bed.

On the floor there we had put some toys in the hopes that the child spirits would come and play with them and hopefully move the chain in the process.

There were two camcorders that were also set up in fixed positions. One camera was in the bedroom on the McClellan side of the house where the ITC session had taken place with my team. The other fixed camcorder was on the first floor of the McClellan side of the house in the room where Jennie's sister had her baby.

The purpose of the cameras are twofold; to simply document the evening and to hopefully catch any possible paranormal activity on video.

The following details some of the evidence we collected that evening using our different video cameras.

DVR Camera in the Second-Floor Bedroom (McClain Side)

✳ Chain begins to move up and down. In this piece of footage you can actually see the chain where the toys were placed moving up and down on its own. At times it looks as though the chain jumps like someone picking at it or trying to pick it up then dropping it.

✳ Light anomaly passes by door frame and down through right quadrant of frame.

✳ A shadow cast against the doorway. Light anomaly passes by camera lens at the same time. The shadow is seen entering the frame from the left hand side where the opening through the wall is made that goes into the McClellan side of the house. The shadow then moves straight across in front of the camera and then disappears.

DVR Camera in the Basement

There were a lot of problems with this camera early on that caused the imaging to go in and out. The exact cause was undetermined. This was in the beginning of the night and not too soon after the spirit of a little girl had said that she was afraid of someone in the basement. The ITC device also failed shortly after the camera did.

✳ A camera moving up and down.

✳ Chain begins to shake vigorously up and down. There is a chain that crosses the room in front of the mannequin and display along the back wall.

✳ Light anomaly passes by camera.

✳ Chain continues to shake up and down.

Digital 8MM Sony in the Second-Floor Bedroom (McClellan Side)

✳ A voice heard: "rod."

✳ Creaks in the room...close up.

✳ Sounds like a small door opening.

✳ Mark seems to hear something. He asks if what he hears is rain. Joe replies, "Yes, it's coming down." You can hear popping in the background... It was a clear night outside... no rain.

✳ Unknown voice says, "wood."

✳ Rappings/knocking (pattern) on floor or wall.

✳ Joe Svehla was using dowsing rods and they started spinning.

✳ Light anomaly crosses past Mark (this could be dust).

✳ Popping sound again in room (possibly rain sound).

✳ Unknown voice says, "You hear that?"

Sony Mini DV in the Second-Floor Bedroom

✳ Deep thud in floor or wall.

✳ Bed creaking.

✳ Carol saying, "Cold spot over here, right behind me."

✳ EMF spike .6.

✳ EMF spike .7 .8.

✳ Carol saying, "I saw a dark shadow over there, too."

Hearin' is Believing

EVP Evidence Transcripts

Kat had also been running her digital voice recorder at the same time that we were using the ITC device recorder. She picked up EVPs that were totally independent of what was recorded on the ITC device.

The following is a transcript of an EVP/ITC session and also what was picked up on the recorder during the session. (The counter notations reflect the location of the anomaly on the digital recorder in minutes and seconds.)

Counter 1:03
"What are your names?"
Response: *creak in floor.*
Response: *"I know who..." (A woman's voice)*

Counter 1:48
"What is your baby's name?"
Response: *"Nathan."*

Counter: 3:22
"What color were the walls in here when you lived here?"
Response: *"I don't know." (whisper)*

Counter: 7:01
"Did you have a child named Lily?"
Response: *"Yes." (whisper)*

Counter: 8:42
"Did children ever come in the house?"
Response: *"Mama" (whisper)*

Counter: 12:27
"Did you like being in this room the most in this house or do you have another room that is your favorite in this house?"
Response: *"Anna or mama." (whisper)*

Counter: 12:51
"Did you used to sit at that desk and write letters?"
No Response.

Counter: 14:12
"How did you feel about the president of the US?"
Response: *"Roosevelt..."*

Counter: 15:23
(Kim says, "The chain is still moving a little bit...")
Response: *"I'm here." (whisper)*

Counter: 18:08
"What is your dog's name?"
Response: *The sounds of Footsteps upstairs are heard.*

Counter: 19:00
"Did you like music?"
Response: *The sound of talking is coming from upstairs.*

Counter: 19:04
"What kind of music did you like?"
Response: *"Mom." (whisper)*

Counter: 19:25
"Did you ever go to the theater?"
Response: *"It's Mom." (whisper)*
Response: *"There's some somebody" (woman's voice)*

"Did you have any favorite plays?"
(Then Kat says, "It sounds like someone whispering…" She is referring to the corner of the room.

Counter: 23:38
"What do you store here in the basement? What do you keep here?"
Response: *"Onions." (whisper)*

Counter: 24:11
"Do you purchase food at the market? Where do you go?"
Response: *"Market." (whisper)*

Counter: 24:31
Response: *Whispers. (Inaudible)*

Counter: 24:55
Response: *"You." (man's voice)*

Counter: 26:29
"They keep a replica of the body here…"
Response: *(Inaudible whisper.)*

Counter: 26:34
"How did you?"
Response: *"Secret."*

Counter: 26:40
"Is this James Wade?"
Response: *"Yes." (whisper)*

Counter: 26:50
Response: *(Inaudible whispers)*

Counter: 27:50
"Is he the one at Eastern State?"
Response: *(Inaudible whispers)*

Counter: 27:53
"Someone's up there…"
Response: *"Hurry" (whisper)*

Counter: 28.12
"Someone's up there…"
Response: *"Love you." (man's voice)*

Kat's sensitivity allowed her to have a greater connection to the spirits she communicated with; it was odd, but somehow the spirits understood or knew that she would hear them and be able to get their message across.

Mark Sarro
DETERMINATIONS

We came away with a great deal of evidence supporting that the Jennie Wade House, in fact, was haunted or had paranormal activity. One of the more difficult things on any investigation is the limited amount of time that you may` spend in the location. In the grand scheme of things, it is really only a small sliver of time in comparison.

Often times, even in the most "haunted" of locations, it can be difficult to gather even a single piece of evidence that would support the claims of the activity being reported. With that said, CCPRS will typically not make any kind of ruling as to whether a location is haunted or has activity based off of a single investigation. For us, the best case scenario is to have a location that we can continue to investigate over a period of time. The opportunity to increase our amount of time spent at the location and to increase the chance for paranormal activity to take place and even potentially gather evidence of that activity on video, audio, or photograph.

It wasn't until the last week of May 2008 that CCPRS would return to Gettysburg to reveal the evidence captured during the investigation of the Jennie Wade House. Bob and I were given the special opportunity to be able to set up and do a taping for our radio show "Voices Carry Paranormal Talk Radio" in the Jennie Wade House during the presentation of evidence. Bob Michaels, Joe, and Karen Svehla were present during the presentation. We revealed the video and audio evidence of the EVPs caught during the ITC sessions and traditional EVP sessions.

The experiences had by myself and the investigators during our investigation of the Jennie Wade house was enough for me to feel that this house was truly haunted. The evidence gathered by CCPRS and by other investigative teams is too great to deny that the house is active with the paranormal.

I urge any enthusiast or someone with simple curiosity on this subject to visit the Jennie Wade House. It is open to the public and history and ghost tours are available during the on and off seasons. The historical implications alone make the home one of interest; and it is something that should be visited and understood.

The Jennie Wade House
548 Baltimore Street
Gettysburg, PA 17325
717-334-4100

Chapter 4

Re-enacting Gettysburg

Rich Hickman

Rich Hickman is a retired police officer and a re-enactor with the 69th Pennsylvania. He is also a member of Delaware County Paranormal Research, a paranormal group based out of Delaware County, Pennsylvania. Rick has had many experiences over the years. The following are a few of his accounts from different places with Gettysburg during his time with the re-enactment group and on investigations with his paranormal group.

A ghostly mist caught at the Triangular Field. Courtesy of Rich Hickman

Rich's Creepy tidbits!

Jennie Wade House

"When I'm in the Jennie Wade basement, I get the "Ickies." It feels like electricity running over my back. It slowly radiates from my shoulders and down my back. I relate it to when you're a kid and you know you did something wrong and you know you're going to get in trouble—that feeling."

Iverson's Pit

"I don't like staying in the Iverson's Pitt area too long. I just don't feel very comfortable there."

East Cavalry Battlefield

"I heard a bugle when I was out at East Cavalry battlefield. It sounded like Officers Call."

Baltimore Street

"I was driving along Baltimore Street and saw a figure cross the road; when I got up to where I saw the figure, it had disappeared."

Farnsworth House

"During an investigation at the Farnsworth House, I was walking out the front door when I was "bumped" by someone. I turned to say "excuse me." But there was no one there."

Culp's Hill

I was up by the tower on Culp's Hill and started to walk down the hill. The road was pretty steep and I slid down on my back. I started to try and get up when I felt hands from behind go under my arms to help me up. There was no one else around me at the time.

Home Sweet Home Motel

Our group of re-enactors were staying at The Home Sweet Home Motel located on the battlefield near where Pickett's men died. At 3am, we were awoken by sounds outside our room. When we got up to check it out, we all heard drums, metal cups, and canteens. It sounded like troop movement, but there was no one outside at that time.

This motel was demolished in February and March of 2003 to restore the battlefield to its 1863 appearance.

Camping In the Rain

I was camped out on July 3rd in Gettysburg. I was woken in the early morning hours by a tremendous rain storm. I glanced at the clock and it was 3am. I went back to sleep and the next morning stepped out of my tent to find it was completely dry outside. Being in the summer, I didn't think too much about it until I was riding into town and remarked to a friend about the hard rain during the night. My friend said that

there was no rain during the night at all. I found that odd until I thought about July 3rd back in 1863 when it rained very hard that evening.

Sach's Bridge

It was November 19, 2006, and I had gone out to Sach's Bridge by myself. It was about 9am and I was alone there. I got out my equipment and spent some time walking around. I didn't have any experiences or get anything unusual on my equipment, so I decided to pack it in. I got back to my truck and got out my cell phone to call home, when I heard a male voice right behind me say, "Hello." There was no one there.

Pickett's Charge

I was participating in the *Living History* weekend at Gettysburg with my group. We were on the battlefield at Pizer's Woods. This is where Pickett's troops lined up to do Pickett's Charge. It was early in the morning and I was dressed in my Union blue uniform. I was walking over to the restrooms and heard some footsteps behind me. I stopped and turned around thinking it was one of our guys there, but there was no one there.

I started walking and once again footsteps followed me. I stopped again and searched for a source for the sounds. There are trees there, but they aren't very big and there wasn't anyone around them.

I started to walk a third time, and the footsteps started again. This time, I stopped and turned around and said, "Look, I don't want to know what regiment you are, I don't want to know how many of you are there, I know I'm wearing the enemy color, but the war was over 130 years ago and I'm going over there to relieve myself and then I'm going back to my camp. I don't want to know what you're doing, I don't want to know anything about you."

With that, I was able to walk on without any more footsteps.

The Angle

While our group of re-enactors were at The Angle, I happened to notice two guys dressed like artillery men standing nearby talking. They didn't notice us and as I looked closer, I thought that these guys really looked authentic. As I glanced away for a moment, then looked back, they had disappeared.

This story happened while we were gathered at our monument located at The Angle. Our group had lost faith in our Captain, and our Lieutenant at the time told him that we no longer wanted him to be our commander. Then a year goes by; we're all assembled once again at Angle.

According to history, General Meagher and his staff gave a sprig of boxwood to every man to wear in his hat to identify them as members of the Irish Brigade. It was now Remembrance Day and we were at the monument giving speeches and saying prayers to honor the fallen.

There was no wind that day, and as we watched the Captain, we saw the sprig of boxwood be lifted by unseen hands from his hat, rise up about four feet above his head, then fall directly to the ground. We couldn't help by think that some of the departed Irish Brigade had the same feelings about this captain.

Chapter 5

More Quick Haunts

Carol Starr
The Baladerry Inn

One of the most haunted inns located in Gettysburg.

This beautiful red brick Federal house was built in 1812 on the Bushman Farm. The rest of the main house was added in 1830. The home was built as a tenant farmers' house and was later occupied by the son of George Bushman. During the battle of Gettysburg, the Bushman Farm was an Army of the Potomac Field hospital. There were additions made in 1972 and 1994 and it was finally converted to a bed and breakfast inn in 1992.

The inn is separated into three different sections, the Main House, the 1812 Section, and the Carriage House. It sits on four beautiful acres near Little Round Top and is surrounded by trees. There is also some history to the ground being the place where Indians were buried.

The first set of stories were given to me by a good friend, Robbin Van Pelt. She has visited The Baladerry Inn many times and has many experiences to share. Robbin is the founder of United States Ghosts Chasers; she is Director of Operations and Photo/Video Analyst for The Maryland Paranormal Investigators Coalition and is Vice-President of Baltimore County Paranormal Research. Robbin uses her skills to help The Baltimore Society of Paranormal Research, Southern Ghost, and The New Jersey Ghost Hunters Society. She has investigated with Mark Nesbitt

Robbin has also appeared on the local major TV stations in Baltimore and in local papers, *The Beltsville News, Capital News* online and *What's Happening Baltimore, FATE* magazine, the TV show *Creepy Canada,* at the *USS Constellation* and Edgar Allan Poe's Grave at the Westminster Catacombs. She filmed an episode for The Discovery Channel at the

This is the carriage house at the Baladerry Inn. There are many stories of paranormal activity in many of the rooms here.

of The Ghosts of Gettysburg fame, Troy Taylor, the author of *The Ghost Hunters Guide Book* and 20 other ghost books, and Rosemary Ellen Guiley, author of *The Encyclopedia of Ghost and Spirits* and 30 other books on the supernatural.

Robbin was published in her first book written by Lynda Lee Macken called *Haunted Baltimore.* She is also in Ed Okonowicz's book, *Baltimore Ghost* and Vince Wilson's *Ghost Tech* and *Ghost Science.* She was in the

Edgar Allan Poe House in Baltimore and is working on writing her own book called *Havre De Grace Hauntings and Legends*. Additionally, Robbin as also helped us (CCPRS) with many investigations.

Robbin's Ghostly Nights Out

Soldiers of Fortune

I was staying at The Baladerry Inn with members from Southern Ghosts. We had the entire place for the weekend. One evening, a couple of us were sitting on the sofa in the main building. We were snapping pictures here and there. One of the pictures that we shot was looking out onto the terrace from the inside. There is a lattice arbor that sits outside and when we all looked at the photo, we could see what looked like two soldiers facing us. They were standing side by side and looked to be pretty solid. They wore black arm bands. I studied the photos and could not find any reason that they would not be authentic. Maybe they were curious as to who was visiting the inn.

The photo is available online at our Web site on our Gettysburg Book page: www.chestercountyprs.com/gburgbook.htm.

An Overnight Drag

Another trip to The Baladerry Inn was in the summertime. I was with several paranormal investigators and we were staying in the Carriage House located separate from the Main House.

During the night, I could hear people talking above me. I also heard sounds like large cabinets were being drug along the floor. This went on from about 2am until 6am. I went upstairs several times to see what was going on, but found the room quiet. The next morning I asked around to see if anyone had also experienced anything and was told that they too had heard talking and furniture dragging, but had assumed it was someone else.

Don't Knock It

On another trip there, I was staying in a ground floor room and around 3am to 4am, I heard knocking coming from the patio doors leading outside. I didn't get up to go check on who or what was out there knocking.

Twin Comfort

In July of 2008, I stayed in the Main House. There is a twin bedroom there. During our visit, we heard music playing and a cat cry. There is a male spirit there also. Things have been moved around in the room and we did get an EVP of a male voice saying "man."

That's Affirmative

Another time I was there with some other paranormal investigators, we were in the Carriage House, and all of a sudden, we could hear talking and/or fighting outside. We got together and took some of our gear with us to go out to investigate. We had recorders,

Main House at the Baladerry Inn where spirits take up residence.

Trifield meters, and a K2 meter. We all heard a man's voice saying "YES."

As we moved around outside asking questions, we heard it once again, but it was coming from another area. We kept moving around and we kept hearing the say male voice saying "YES." It happened a total of five times. We also had spikes on the Trifield meter.

Out With a Bang!

On another visit, I was in a downstairs room and started to hear banging sounds like someone banging on a car hood or on a trash can. There were others staying there that also reported hearing these noises in the middle of the night.

Spirits Prefer Blondes

It was late one evening, and I thought I'd pack up my gear and such to be ready to leave in the morning. It was around 4am and I had just finished up doing some investigations. I was standing there packing up my gear and clothes. All of a sudden, I felt a pinch or a bite on the back of my leg. I had on long pants and I thought maybe it was some sort of bug. Then again, I felt it, and this time even harder, so I pulled down my pants to check for bites or red marks, but didn't see anything. At this time, one of the other investigators told me that the spirit that was in that room liked blonde-haired women, and at that time, I had lighter hair.

The Baladerry Inn
40 Hospital Road
Gettysburg, Pennsylvania
Owner – Suzanne Lonky

GHOST SOLDIER JEREMIAH BOYLE?

CCPRS Investigator and author Dinah Roseberry remarks, "It's only natural that Gettysburg and its ghosts have feelers out to other areas of Pennsylvania. Men and women loyal to the state made their ways to this historic town for many reasons, though battle was the most traumatic... And they sometimes made their ways back to their own hometowns in Pennsylvania after dying on the fields of Gettysburg."

One such soldier just might be Jeremiah Boyle, who enlisted as a Sergeant on October 31, 1861, with Company H, 69th Infantry—and died in battle. Oddly, it just so happens that he might also be the ghost who frequents the Mansion House Tavern on East Bridge Street in Phoenixville, Pennsylvania.

Historic researcher and ancestry analyst Bradford Williams became intrigued with the story of Jeremy at the tavern related in Roseberry's book, *Ghosts of Valley Forge and Phoenixville*. From the book about the Mansion House:

It began some years ago when a blind woman came with her husband to enjoy the food provided by the House. And where were they seated? Table Two, of course!

The woman said to the server, "Do you know that you have ghosts here?"

The server (and everyone else on staff) did, indeed, know of the ghosts even then, and told the woman about the ghost of Table Two. But the woman frowned up at the server with blind eyes.

"No," she said pointing to a serving station at a nearby area by the kitchen. "He is over there by the side station." It was wondered by staff then—and staff now—how a blind woman even knew that there was what they called a "side station" where she'd pointed. The woman's husband took her by the arm and led her to the station, where she had about a twenty minute conversation with the ghost.

One of the Mansion House ghosts was identified through this encounter. The ghost, Jeremy, told the blind woman that he was a Civil War soldier who had been killed at the age of twenty-one. He described himself as six-foot-two with blond hair and blue eyes.

A sweet story, to be sure. Researcher Williams told Roseberry:

I was intrigued by your Mansion House story and the ghost of Civil War soldier Jeremy. I decided to look for Jeremy in the genealogy world amongst the Civil War records I have access to. I found about eight Jeremys having served for Pennsylvania, with none of them listed as having been killed in battle or dying while serving. Next, I searched "Jeremiah" and received 1,202 matches for those serving for Pennsylvania. Just looking through the first 100 matches alphabetically (A and part of B last names), I found one drowned, five died, one died from disease, one died from wounds, and one killed. One of the two killed would be more likely, as he was killed at Gettysburg on July 8, 1863.

Jeremiah Boyle, enlisted in Philly as a Sergeant on 10/31/1861 with Company H - 69th Infantry.

Jeremiah's marker can be found in section D, grave 8.

Roseberry continues:

So has this particular soldier who died and was buried in Gettysburg returned home to haunt a favorite place where the memories are not so harsh? The Mansion House served as an inn and to furnish food, drink, and lodging for travelers in that time period, as well as now. Perhaps those, like Jeremy, who died in battle prefer to stay at a kinder and merrier place in eternity, rather than continuing to fight the Battle of Gettysburg over and over.

This ghost interacts with those around him. He's happy to be at the Mansion House… and I for one, hope he never has to return to the day of his death.

For those interested in visiting the Phoenix Mansion House in Phoenixville, Pennsylvania, to see where this Gettysburg ghost story begins, enjoy the spirits at this fine restaurant located at 37 Bridge Street, Phoenixville, PA 19460. Telephone: 610-933-9962.

Carol Starr
SACH'S BRIDGE

Sach's Bridge was built in 1852. Over the years, it has been the site of many things, such as a flood in 1996, but in July of 1863, it was used by retreating Confederate soldiers fleeing back to Virginia.

To this day, the bridge stands as a reminder of the many men who marched over it, some wounded and dying, and the many emotions trapped there.

This beautiful covered bridge has been witness to retreating confederate soldiers.

Looking through Sachs Bridge. This bridge was used as an escape route
for confederate soldiers retreating back to Virginia.

A Way Home

May 29, 2008

I had always heard about Sach's Bridge, but had not gotten a chance to visit it until recently. I went out there with another investigator, Kim Ritchie, and we spent a lot of time on the bridge and walking around the grounds around it.

After we crossed over the bridge and walked down the trail, we decided to have a seat near the waterfall. It was a beautiful day and no one else was out there. We had our recorders on and took many pictures with our digital cameras. We then started to walk back towards the bridge and Kim was asking questions while holding her K2 meter. (A K2 meter is a type of EMF meter. Instead of showing a digital read out, it uses a series of lights to show the levels of electric and magnetic fields. We use it in the field by asking questions. Prior to asking a question, you would instruct the spirit to please light up 1 light for yes and 2 lights for no.)

All of a sudden, she stopped and the lights on the K2 began flashing.

For the next few minutes we stood there asking questions and getting responses from the meter. The EMF meter was also spiking during this period. After a couple of minutes, the EMF went back down to 0 and the K2 meter went silent. Could this have been a lost soldier trying to find his way back home? We both wondered if perhaps this was a soldier from the south passing by us as he was retreating from the battle on his was back to Virginia.

A photo looking from the bridge showing the reflection into the water.

A beautiful scene from Sachs Bridge.

Chapter 6
Triangular Field

Carol Starr
Southern Gentlemen

I was attending a paranormal conference in Gettysburg with members of Chester County Paranormal Research Society. After the conference, my friend and fellow investigator, Kim Ritchie, and I decided to drive around the battlefield. We drove up to Little Round Top, Devils Den, and then pulled over across from Triangular Field. Getting out of the car, we walked through the wooden gate, entering the path down to the woods.

As we started to walk, we asked if there were any southern gentlemen with us. And was this any way a southern gentleman treats a lady? We had hoped for a greeting, but this was just a half-hearted gesture on our part.

We continued asking questions until we walked all the way down to the bottom and back up to the vehicle.

It was after 9pm by then and we knew we needed to be out of the park by 10pm. We got into the vehicle and slowly starting moving down the road. Every now and then, we would pull over to take pictures of monuments and the woods. We pulled over not far from the field and sat quietly looking out into the darkness.

Suddenly as we looked to the front left side of the vehicle, we saw a white mist appear out of nowhere. And walking out of the mist was a tall figure. Stunned,

A stone wall that runs through Triangular Field.

71

we were frozen as the figure brushed by the driver's side window and continued to the back left side window before dissolving back into the mist.

I'd seen, from shoulder to waist, the wool steel gray uniform of a Confederate officer. Only then did Kim and I turn to look at each other. Our eyes were the size of saucers and I knew she had witnessed the same thing as I had.

I said, "I think that was our southern gentleman!"

I do believe that someone heard us out there in the field and wanted to make sure the ladies were treated to a southern gentleman's charm.

This old wooden gate is the entrance to Triangular Field.
Many people have reported equipment failure once they passed this point.

Carol Starr

Footsteps from Behind

We visited Triangular Field in the afternoon. All of us were shocked at seeing that the field had been cleared of the trees that were originally located at the bottom of the field. Everything was wide open now.

Kim Ritchie and I started to walk down the path towards the bottom of the hill. As we were walking, I could hear heavy footsteps right behind us, so I was assuming that Mark Sarro had followed us down. Talking about the previous time we had been there, I turned around to talk to Mark... and came to a dead stop. Mark was sitting way back at the top of the hill.

I looked at Kim and asked, "Didn't you hear someone walking behind us?"

She said advised that, yes; that to her, it sounded like marching right behind us.

This photo shows the tree line going down through Triangular Field. In recent years, the area has been brought back to the way it looked during the battle. Ghostly soldiers have been seen at the edge of the trees.

We continued to walk around the bottom of the field, and then started back up to meet up with Mark and Kat.

As we got back up to the top of Triangular Field, I asked Mark, if he had seen me turn around and look behind me; he said, "Yes." So I told him what had happened and what we had heard. I think we had been followed down the path by a curious spirit.

Chapter 7

The Wheatfield

Carol Starr
A Brief History

The Wheatfield consists of twenty acres of land near The Peach Orchard. This small patch of land was witness to much bloodshed and violence during the three-day battle. The battle on the afternoon of July 2nd left this field and nearby woods strewn with more than 4,000 dead and wounded Union and Confederate soldiers.

It is said that after the battle, you could not walk across the field and touch earth, there were so many bodies.

Today, this area is a beautiful area to visit, but on many of our visits, it gave us glimpses of what occurred on those summer days back in 1863.

Mark Sarro
My Impressions

The Wheatfield is a place of much despair and agony. So many men were left to lay dying on that field as the result of the bloody battle that transpired there. Every time I visit the Wheatfield, I can't help but have the sense that everywhere I step and turn lay a man wounded and dying. It is almost as though I can hear them calling out. The imprint of

This is the High Water Mark at Pickett's Charge.

A close up of the flame
on top of the monument.

This monument was visited by President John Kennedy and his wife, Jackie, prior to his assassination.

their sorrow is thick upon the ground. I am not a sensitive or medium of any sorts, but for some reason when I step onto the Wheatfield that is the sensation inside me.

I have taken many photographs of the Wheatfield and have even gotten down to ground level to take a picture, expecting to catch a soldier on film reaching out for help. The first time I stepped onto that ground, I did not know all of the details of what had happened there, but I knew that there was an energy present that, at times, seemed to be overwhelming.

SHADOW IN THE FIELD

It was after dark on that hot summer night in July of 2006 when I had one of many experiences at the Wheatfield in Gettysburg. I had been in town for a paranormal conference that was being held nearby at the Holiday Inn. Isaac, Michele, Kat, and I had decided to visit the battlefield after a long day of lectures and seminars at the conference.

We arrived at the Wheatfield just as the last remnant of the sun was setting down beyond the horizon. It was dusk, but now getting dark. We had all started off together, but had started to separate a little. The field, by this time, was thick and high with the growth left untouched since spring. There were several paths cut out in the field that led to the center where the monuments stood.

Major General Governor K. Warren's statue keeps watch over the Valley of Death.

I turned and saw what appeared to be a tall figure standing in the field; it was already dark, but still I could see that there was something or someone there. I moved a step closer in the direction to where it stood, and in that instant, it shot off across the field and disappeared.

I knew then that it was not one of my colleagues, and by its lack of form and definition, that it was in fact a shadow person.

What is a Shadow Person? Where do they come from? There are many theories and speculations about the nature of shadow people. This was not the first time that I would come face to face with a shadow person. In my first book, *Ghosts of West Chester* (Pennsylvania), I dedicate an entire section of stories to shadow people and the experiences that I have personally had with them, as well as those had by others. I define a shadow person as follows in my book:

General Oliver Howard's monument.

The view from Little Round Top.

There is theory that the "Shadow person" is the ephemeral body of someone who is astral projecting. A lot of these reported phenomena have happened as something that is seen from the corner of the eye at the edge of peripheral vision, while still others report seeing it straight on.

The Shadow people are different then ghosts or spirits because of their lack of definition and detail. They are by their very nature a shadow or outline of a human form. One of the common features that has been reported on these creatures is that of having glowing red eyes. This in itself can be disturbing because yet another theory portends that it is that of a demonic or subhuman nature. (Of all the experiences that I have had with this phenomena, I have never seen the glowing red eyes as reported in so many other cases.) Are these demonic beings or are they the astral body of a traveler passing through?

The questions remained—what was this figure at the Wheatfield?

29th Pennsylvania Infantry. This is across from the 2nd Maryland Monument.

Carol Starr

The Stranger

I was, again, with Investigator Kim Ritchie, when we decided to venture out in The Wheatfield. It was getting dark and we started to walk deeper into the field. Just the two of us were there and I noticed that, as we walked, I could hear footsteps about twenty feet away walking with us.

We were on the path, so the footsteps were coming from the un-mowed area. We would stop. The footsteps would stop. We would start to walk again and we could hear the footsteps next to us.

We walked back to the New York monument and put our gear down. It was a beautiful, peaceful evening. Soon, however, we were in almost complete darkness. We could only see a couple of feet away with our small flashlights.

Suddenly, Kim said she saw someone approaching from one side of the monument. I turned my flashlight in that area and soon noticed what looked to be a man walking towards us. Now, it is usually the norm to announce yourself when traveling out there in the dark. This person said nothing. He continued to approach us, then stopped at the back of the monument and looked up for a few seconds as if to read the words. It was so dark, we could only make out that it was a man. We couldn't make out any features.

A monument dedicated to Col. Patrick O'Rourke.
They say if you rub his nose, you will have good luck!

79

After a moment, he started to walk away and headed back towards the road. He said nothing, and within a few seconds, he was completely gone. We went over the area with our flashlights, but saw nothing. A few minutes later a young couple walked up to us. We started to talk to them and eventually asked them if they had seen a man walk past them. They said they hadn't seen anyone out there until they happened upon us.

Was this mysterious man real or was he someone from the past paying tribute to the fallen out there in the night at The Wheatfield?

CCPRS investigators Carol Starr and Dinah Roseberry heard a lone bugler playing *Taps* from this point late one summer evening.

When walking through this field, you can sometimes hear footsteps following you.

Carol Starr

GUNPOWDER

On another trip to Gettysburg, I went out to The Wheatfield with a couple of our investigators. We split up and went to different areas around the field. I picked an area under a tree on the right hand side of the field. I sat down and turned on my recorder. After sitting there enjoying the quiet, I started to smell something. After a few minutes, I realized that is was gunpowder. It only lasted about a minute or two, then it disappeared.

About fifteen minutes later, I smelled it again. The field was very quiet; it was mid afternoon, and no breeze, but I knew that it was something left over from a battle fought there many years before.

81

Carol Starr

The Bugle

In July 2007, I attended a ghost conference in Gettysburg along with investigator and author Dinah Roseberry. After a day at the conference, we were both eager to get out to the battlefield and explore after dark. We decided to go to The Wheatfield. We got there around dusk, approximately 9pm, and walked up to the New York monument in the back center of the field.

We didn't notice anyone else there in the field and we were taking this quiet time to wind down after a long day. We watched the sun disappear and the woods grow darker and darker.

As I stood there, considering what life might have been like just prior to that horrible day in July all those years ago, I started to hear something coming from the woods about 100 yards in front of us. I looked at Dinah and asked if she was hearing it also. She said no, so I started to hum along with the tune I was hearing. It was a lone bugle, sad and tearful in sound, and as I was humming, Dinah suddenly announced that not only could she hear it now, too, but that it was "Taps!"

She jumped up beside me and we both stood there facing the woods listening to the bugle playing a mournful end to the day. Tears welled in our eyes as the music faded into nothingness.

When we went back to town, we asked around to see if there possibly was a group out there camping or an event taking place that might be cause for the lonely vigil of that bugler, but were told that no one was there. We were alone in the darkness, taking in all the sadness that the Wheatfield had to offer that night.

Hearing this lone tune coming out of the darkness really affected me. Could it have been to mourn the lives lost on the battlefield so long ago? Or was it just a symbol of what each night brought to this field in Gettysburg? All I know is that those who listen to the phantom bugler feel the same weariness of the soldiers long past.

Carol Starr

The Whistle

On June 18, 2006, I was with another investigator and we decided to head over to The Wheatfield to see if we could catch anything with our equipment. It was about 11:15am and it was a hot 92 degrees. We were alone out in the Wheatfield and started to hike up the pathway. We used our EMF meters, cameras, thermometers, and recorders. At the top of the path, near the New York monument, my friend stopped to get something out of her bag. We then continued on through the field taking down information and data readings. After we returned home, we listened to our audio recordings and had a strange sound come over the recording. It occurred when my friend had stopped at the top of the path and bent down to get something out of her bag.

On the recording you hear a distinct whistle. It was very loud and clear, although, we did not hear it.

Was it someone whistling in the hot weather for a cool drink? Or a warning to a soldier of long ago? It will always remain a mystery.

Mark Sarro

ON THE HILLSIDE

It was one of our first visits to Gettysburg in 2006 when we were on the road alongside the Wheatfield; a small brick wall ran the length of the road and a line of trees ran along the top of the hill, on just the

A photograph of The Pennsylvania Monument.

other side was the Wheatfield. We were in the car, and Kat asked for us to stop the car. She felt that something was near and going on up the hill. Not one to stand back to wait for an invitation, she got out of the car and began to make her way up the hill.

One by one we began to follow her. She stepped over the wall and began to walk towards the line of trees. I was not too far behind her, taking pictures as we went.

"I just heard a woman crying! Right behind me!" I said, as I looked at Kat. "Did you hear it?"

"No. Where was it?" She asked.

"It was right here, it felt like it was right behind me!" I turned and motioned to the general area within my reach.

She began to make her way back down towards me and then stopped. It was in that moment that we both heard what sounded like a horse whinnying as though it were right next to us.

"I just heard a horse. Did you hear that?" I asked.

"Yes, I did." She remarked, her eyes wide.

"It seemed like it was right next to us. Did it sound that way to you too?" I asked.

"Yes, it did."

She came closer to me and we made our way back down the hill and towards the car.

That was one of the early experiences that I had in Gettysburg. It was interesting because the sounds were as though they were right next to me, yet there was no woman and there was no horse there. It happened so quickly, and the way that it sounded, it could not have been a sound carried to us from some distance. It was too near, it sounded too close to be something like that. Was it a residual energy? I can't say for sure. But I know what I heard...

Chapter 8

Psychic Intervention

Laurie Hull

Laurie Hull is the founder and director of Delaware County Paranormal Research—she is also a psychic medium. The paranormal haunts Laurie whether she wants it to or not. Living in Springfield, Pennsylvania, she has had a lifelong interest in ghosts and the supernatural that began while she was growing up in a haunted house. She has been interviewed about the paranormal for local and national radio and television shows and  newspapers. Laurie has traveled throughout the United States and England, Ireland, and France to investigate haunted places. Her extensive research and photographs have been referenced in books and Web sites about the paranormal.

We hope you enjoy the following stories from Laurie's archives of haunted Gettysburg.

The Comfort Inn

871 York Road
Gettysburg, PA 17325
(717) 337-2400

No Rest for the Weary

The first time I visited Gettysburg, I ended up at the Comfort Inn because it was the first place I found with a vacancy. My stay there was so pleasant that I decided to book a room there when I returned. During the second stay, I was given a room on the ground floor in the wing closest to York Road. I was a bit worried because there seemed to be a lot of guests there and I imagined hearing people walking around overhead all night long.

As it turned out, I needn't have worried about that. I was exhausted from working all day and then driving the two hours to Gettysburg. I just wanted to get a shower and go to sleep to rest up for a full day of battlefield exploration the next day. I think I fell asleep as soon as I hit the bed.

What seemed like a few minutes later, I was wide awake. There was someone standing next to my bed, looking down at me! Afraid to move or even breathe, I froze under the blanket, waiting to die.

To my horror, he began to lean over me. Suddenly, my mouth and nose felt like I was breathing in water. I struggled to breathe and realized there was no air getting into in my mouth and nose and the shadowy figure was gone. Somehow, I was able to sit up and began coughing and catching my breath.

After a few minutes, I convinced myself it was a dream and fell back asleep, only to wake up to the same shadowy figure followed by what I can only describe as some type of attack, where once again, I couldn't breathe. This time, I went back to sleep with the light on. The light didn't help because it happened again. I ended up getting absolutely no sleep at all that night. In the morning, I asked the hotel staff to please move my room. They did, without question. Looking back, that is slightly odd, unless people regularly experienced problems in that room.

What or who was the figure by my bed that night? I have no answer for that question. It has never happened since, but when I have stayed at that hotel, I've made sure my room was not in that section. I have often heard that the entire Gettysburg area is haunted. This experience showed me that not even new buildings are immune to ghostly manifestations.

The Haunted Hotel Room

I was excited to be going to Gettysburg for St. Patrick's day weekend. I arrived at my hotel late in the evening only to find out that my room had been given out and the hotel was booked solid. I was happy to locate an available room at the Comfort Inn located on Route 30 just outside of town. I checked into room 103 and was asleep by midnight.

I was having a dream about something coming toward me when, all of a sudden, I woke up! This wasn't a dream at all. I was feeling invisible hands on my throat and was struggling to breath. I looked up and saw a glowing yellowish form on top of me. Within seconds, the form and the invisible hands disappeared and I was once again alone in my bed.

A Soldier

During another visit, I walked over towards a bridge near the Comfort Inn Hotel. I wanted to check my batteries, so I sat down near the bridge.

I suddenly saw a figure of a young Confederate soldier. I found that I could communicate with him and he said he wasn't sad. He also wasn't sure what year it was or how much time had passed. I asked him about what he thought about the cars that were around and he said that he saw them, but didn't know what they were. He said that I reminded him of his sister. I told him that he could hang out with us.

I probably shouldn't have said that considering he followed us through Gettysburg... and then also followed us to my home. At my house, I would glimpse him at the bottom of my stair steps. I told him it was alright for him to come up the stairs, but he said, "That just wasn't right." He followed me everywhere.

About two weeks later, I was hanging out with the bartenders at the General Wayne Inn. We were discussing past lives. One of them looked at me and said that every time he looked at me, he saw a Confederate soldier. The soldier also followed me to a birthday party. I have a picture from the party showing an orb where I saw him standing.

He seemed to me as being from the deep south, possibly either Alabama or Arkansas, and he was very young looking—probably around seventeen or eighteen years old. He was very nice and polite and he felt very sorry for the south.

I was attending college, and one day I saw him standing by a window at the school, and he suddenly looked away. I asked him if he saw someone out there. He looked surprised. He then turned back to me and said that he had to go.

I haven't seen the young southern soldier since, but I am hoping that he has found peace.

JENNIE WADE HOUSE AND THE ORPHANAGE

I was attending a ghost conference in 2001 in Gettysburg and visited the Jennie Wade House. As I walked through the house, I noticed the chains swinging in the upstairs bedroom. As I walked down the stairs, a coldness followed me. When I went down into the basement, I felt as though a spirit was responding and evolving. I felt that I was chasing something throughout the house.

I also visited the Orphanage basement. The girl who was next to me was taking the temperature when I noticed the temperature dropping.

Were we alone? I don't think so.

SPANGLER SPRING

I have been to Spangler Spring many times.

A Death of Batteries

One night I was walking up the hill behind the spring. I had all of my equipment with me and was ready to take some pictures. I got up to the top of the hill when my camera batteries died. I walked back down to get new batteries and again walked back up to the top of the hill. As soon as I got up there, the batteries died once again. I walked back down to the car and took all my new batteries up with me to the top of the hill. I replaced the batteries with the brand new ones and once again, they all died. At this point I just threw up my hands and announced, "You win!" and went back to the hotel.

A Spooky Walk

In March the following year, I went back to Spangler Spring. It was very dark when we arrived and we started to walk around the area and up the hill. I started to hear someone walking near us. It was very dark, so I called out, "Is someone out there?" I didn't want to have another group stumble out of the woods on us, so I again called out to see if there were others nearby. I didn't get a response.

But we again heard walking. The terrain around this area was extremely rocky and in the pitch dark, there was no way someone could be walking out there without a flashlight.

We started to hear heavy footsteps. I noted that the ground was covered with leaves that made a distinctive crunching noise when walked on. The footsteps that we were hearing were very clear with no crunching noises.

We all decided to leave this spirit alone in the woods.

SLAUGHTER PEN

A Soldier's Desperation

On my first trip to Gettysburg, I ended up in the area that I am told is the "slaughter pen." This visit coincided with some kind of ghost convention, and in my efforts to avoid the throng of people that had invaded Devil's Den, I walked across the way into the woods. There were two friends with me that night and we were all excited about our first night on the battlefield.

One of my friends was familiar with the battlefield, so he was pointing out different areas of the woods and told us which regiments would have been in which areas. I heard him talking about where a Union regiment that he was interested in would have been, and I began to wander off in search of a hot spot (an area where I felt that subtle change in the atmosphere that tells me a ghost is there).

It was very dark and I was trying to avoid tripping over the large rocks that dot the landscape there. I heard a noise directly in front of me and I stopped to listen.

Nothing.

I began walking again, this time more slowly. There it was again!

I stopped again. Silence…

I went to take a step and I heard it again, right ahead of me behind some large boulders. I turned on my audio recorder and began walking towards the sounds.

"Are you over here?" I asked as I climbed over the boulder.

As soon as I landed on the other side, I felt a strong presence with me and I dropped to a crouch. I felt like there was someone right next to me—but I wasn't seeing anything. After checking to make sure my recorder was still on, I began to ask questions.

This area lies between Little Round Top and Devils Den. Many lives were lost here during the battle. Countless sightings of soldiers wandering through here still looking for the battle.

"What is your name? What can I do to help you?"

Suddenly my friends started shouting to me, "Come over here, they're over here!"

I knew they must have been experiencing something, but so was I, and I didn't want to leave. I turned back toward where I thought the presence was and pointed the microphone towards it.

Before I could ask a question, One of my friends yelled again, "You have to see this!" as he was walking towards me. The atmosphere got very tense where I was and I felt that the approach of my friend was disturbing this ghost that was next to me. I stood up and called out, "All right, give me a minute. I'm coming."

I came out from behind the boulder and went over to see what all the fuss was about. At that time, digital cameras were the latest thing and he was waving me over to see a photo he had taken that showed a misty shape.

"See!" he said excitedly, "I told you this part of the battlefield was good."

I didn't know how really good it was until the next day when I was reviewing my recording. Right after my friend yelled out, "They're over here!", there was a man's voice on my recording. It had a very strong southern accent and what it said gave me chills.

The voice said, "I'll shoot you."

Intrigued by the recording, this area of the park was the spot I focused on during my return visit to Gettysburg the next year. Once again, the town was full of ghost enthusiasts. Apparently, someone had spread the word about the slaughter pen woods because there were a lot of people tramping around in there.

Although I was again accompanied by two friends, I decided to walk off by myself into the woods. I started recording, hoping to capture another voice like I had the year before. I heard footsteps off to my right. I didn't think anything of it, and continued with my EVP session, asking questions like, "Is there anyone here who would like to talk?"

I took a few photos, and as I snapped the last one, I noticed someone right in front of me. Immediately, I began to apologize for blinding this person with my flash, when I realized who, or rather *what* it was.

There was a man in dark clothing and a hat passing by. The air around me fell still and silent, voices faded into the background, and it seemed like time itself stopped. He was staring straight ahead, off to my left and he was walking with a purpose in his step. He walked right on by like I was not even there; he never even changed the rhythm of his step during the time I observed him. As I was watching him walk, he was suddenly gone, and I felt like the world started again. It had been so quiet in the brief seconds I saw him walking that everything seemed jarring and loud now.

I started crying and was so overcome with a feeling of deep depression and hopelessness that I walked back to the car and sat there. When my friends noticed I was in the car, they came over to ask me what was wrong. I couldn't explain it, so I said I just wanted to leave. Truly, I did want to leave. The feelings I was experiencing were so intense and disturbing that I needed to get out of there.

After traveling to Gettysburg so many times in the hopes of capturing some evidence of ghosts or experiencing some profound paranormal event, I should have been excited by what I had seen. For some reason, I was not. During that short experience, and each time I reflect on it, I am so overcome by a feeling of sadness and hopelessness.

After we returned to the hotel that night, I lost all interest in further investigation and just wanted to go back to my home. I didn't return to the battlefield that weekend. I couldn't.

I am not sure why I felt so sad, or why I'd hoped never see him again. Was it because I'd picked up on the feelings of a long-dead soldier? Was it because I felt so sad for that man, lost somewhere in time and space, compelled to attempt and re-attempt to complete a mission he will never complete?

If I ever do see him again, maybe I can get some answers. Until that time, or until the end of *my* time, I pray for his soul's peace.

One More Visitor

At another time, while I was attending a paranormal conference, I went out to the woods behind Devils Den to the Slaughter Pen. I was alone and there weren't too many people in the woods. I took two pictures and at the second flash, I saw a man standing there in front of me. I went to say, "I'm sorry," when he started walking towards me. I found it very odd that as he walked toward me, and then pass by me, he never turned his head. He was dressed in a dark uniform, hat, brim, and coat. As he passed me, I had this intense feeling of loss, depression, and wanting to die.

I left the area and sat in the car. I wanted to just go home. I felt as if he was going somewhere, felt utter sadness, that his soul was trapped. I felt as though I'd accidentally dug up a grave.

I can't bring myself to visit that area again.

SACH'S BRIDGE

Sach's Bridge is a truly haunted place. Visitors to the bridge have heard unexplained sounds, voices, and footsteps. Photos taken there almost always contain some kind of anomaly. Audio recordings there reveal unexplained voices, or EVPs, on playback. The bridge itself and the path on the Park side of the bridge have always been distinctly colder than the temperature in other areas. The whole bridge and the fields around it have the heavy atmosphere feeling that is common in haunted places.

Built in 1854 by David Stoner, Sachs Covered Bridge crosses Marsh Creek. It is on the edge of the Battlefield Park. During the War, the bridge was known as Sauck's Bridge, and is located about one mile behind Warfield's Ridge, not far behind the right flank of the Confederate artillery line which participated in the pre-charge barrage of July 3, 1863. Portions of the Confederate Army used the bridge to cross Marsh Creek during the July 3rd and July 4th withdrawal from Gettysburg.

It is said that Rebel deserters who were hung from the rafters here. There are rumors of unmarked and undiscovered mass graves in the surrounding fields. All of those things combine to form the perfect place to encounter a ghost.

I have heard the footsteps and taken many photos there that contained unusual features that I could not explain.

Camera Shy

I was out at Sach's Bridge with two other people when we saw someone walking out of the bridge. We were there taking pictures and I was about to say sorry about taking pictures as he was walking in front of us... when he just disappeared.

When it Rains, It Pours

A man in the 69th Irish Regiment was camped out at the bridge. He was sitting up late at night listening to the pouring rain. When he got up in the morning, he noticed that it was completely dry outside. He asked around to see if anyone else was kept up by the pouring rain during the night, but was told that it hadn't rained that night.

Always Speak When Spoken To...Or Else

One afternoon, when I took my children to visit the bridge, my youngest daughter got bored and strayed a little ways into the field to pick flowers.

We were calmly walking around and enjoying the bright sunny afternoon when she began screaming and flailing at the air around her. Thinking that she had disturbed a hornet nest or something I rushed over.

People have seen ghostly apparitions marching through the bridge.

She was crying out and swatting the air—but there was nothing there.

I picked her up and I noticed the air around her was like ice. Not sure what was going on, we went back to the car and drove as fast as we could out of there. We stopped to get her some ice cream and to ask her what had happened. I was still thinking maybe she saw some kind of large insect or something.

Well, what she saw couldn't have been an insect.

She said she was just picking flowers (dandelions) and she heard someone say her name. Thinking it was one of her sisters trying to scare her, she just ignored it. All of a sudden, she said it got really cold and she saw all these little white things flying around her. She said she tried to walk away but they all came in front of her.

I asked her, "Were they bugs?"

She said, "I don't think so. I didn't see any wings, and anyway bugs don't talk and they don't like the cold. These things were talking."

"They were talking?" I asked in shock.

So what else is in Gettysburg, besides the spirits of soldiers?

PA Monument

When I visited the monument, I smelled cigar/pipe smoke.

Sniper Hole/Devils Den

A Moving Story

On my first visit to Gettysburg, (more years ago than I want to admit), I was given a tour of the battlefield by one of my friends who lived in the area. He told me about the heavy fighting that happened in the Devil's Den area and of the ghosts of Union and Confederate soldiers that have been seen there. Part of this tour of Devil's Den included the famous "Sniper's Hole."

The legend was began with the publication of a photograph:

"The photograph captioned, 'Home of a Rebel Sharpshooter,' in Gardner's book, *Gardner's Photographic Sketch Book of the War,* shows the dead sniper lying on his back, his face turned toward the camera, and his rifle propped up against one of the rocks. The image would have remained a striking photographic document if it were not for another picture that shows the same soldier in a different location. This photograph is a closer view of the young

Located at the bottom of the rock formations.

man still lying on his back, but his face is turned away from the camera and his rifle lies on the ground by his side. Apparently, the frustration with using slow films and lenses that made it impossible to photograph action during the battle induced the photographer to create his own dramatic picture. In order to create the picture, he and his assistant dragged the dead body of Pvt. Hoge from the field where he fell over to the hole."

Another part of the legend, as mentioned in the first story of the hole, is that it is said that no one can take a picture of the sniper's hole. This is usually attributed to the spirit of the fallen soldier, who resented his image being used in this way. He now haunts the area, interfering with cameras and making it impossible to take any photos there.

On this trip, I was able to take many photos of the hole and also on subsequent visits, so I put the legend of the camera-shy Confederate soldier down to legend.

No Photos Please

Several years after my first visit, I took my children to Gettysburg and gave them the whole tour of the battlefield, complete with all the ghost stories I knew as well as all of the experiences I have had there.

As I stood in front of the Sniper's Hole, telling them the legend of the camera-shy Confederate soldier, I turned to take a photograph to show them that the legend is not true. I pointed the lens towards the hole and when I went to take the photo my camera suddenly flew out of my hand, up in the air and landed about three feet away. For the first time that day the kids were completely silent. I picked up the camera, silently apologized to the ghost.

"I thought you said there was no ghost there," said my youngest daughter.

"As far as I knew there wasn't," was all I could say to her.

The air around us seemed charged and expectant, as is usually the case when a ghost makes its presence known. It seemed like he was waiting for me to do or say something. If I hadn't been standing there with my three young daughters, I would have tried to get to the bottom of the event. The concerned and slightly frightened looks on their faces told me it was time to go.

Why had that happened? It occurred to me that this was the first time I had actually stood there and

Another scenic photograph of Devils Den where snipers hid.

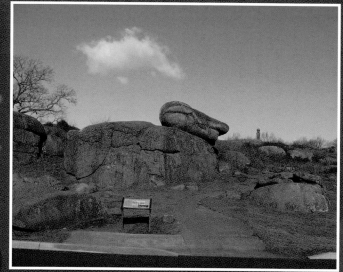

A photograph of Devils Den. Many have seen ghostly soldiers roam the rocks where snipers hid during the battle.

told the story to someone. Why was he trying to get my attention? Was it something I said? All the way home it bothered me. Could there be another reason besides the one we had heard for the ghost to hang around the "Sniper's Hole?" Was there another story out there?

Hidden snipers would pick off the enemy up on
Little Round Top from here.

...And the Plot Thickens

I published our experience on our Web site and hoped that I would get some feedback. About a year went by before I received an inquiry about it. It was from a college professor and he wanted to bring my attention to another side of the story.

He was doing research on the topic of this sharpshooter, and had uncovered some interesting information. He agreed that while the man in the photo has traditionally been identified as Andrew Hoge, this identification was based on the statement of a person who knew Hoge and thought that the man in the photo was him. This identification is a marginal note with the photo in the Library of Congress Archives.

97

Frassanito's case for this identification can be read here: http://memory.loc.gov/ammem/cwphtml/cwpcam/cwcam3.html

However, while Andrew Hoge did die at Gettysburg, he was with the *4th* Virginia infantry and most likely fell at Culp's Hill. The Confederate regiments who died in the area of the Sniper's Hole were the same rebels who attacked Devil's Den and Little Round Top—the regiments from Texas and Alabama. The whole case for an alternate identity of the camera-shy Confederate was outlined by Jim Groves at http://www.jamescgroves.com/henry/summary.htm.

Maybe when the truth about his identity is confirmed, he will be able to rest in peace.

After the battle, many dead soldiers were found among these rocks.

Chapter 9

Mark Sarro

The Soldiers History Museum/The Orphanage

A Brief History

The Soldiers History museum was started by Charlie Weaver in the 1950s. The museum remains much the same as it was then. Upon entering the museum, you are immediately in the gift shop that opens up and continues to the back of the building; to the right are the exhibits—display cases full of weapons, miniatures of battlefields, and full size mannequins depicting various scenes. To the right of the gift shop is an open pit with the mannequin of a small boy that peers up at you as you look down upon him. This museum is the original building that once was the orphanage.

The story goes that a dead Union soldier was found clutching a picture of his three children. It was so compelling, the photograph soon circulated and the search for his wife and family began. The orphanage was started for the purpose of taking in the orphan children of those who had died from the Civil War.

The original matron of the orphanage was a woman who had lost her husband to the war. She came to live there with her own children. During her time there,

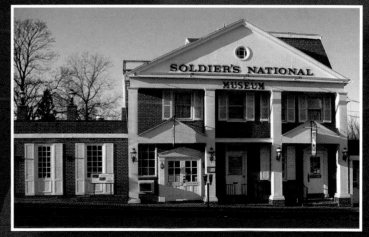

This is a photo of the Soldiers Museum and Orphanage located on Baltimore Street.

the orphanage was under the care of a loving woman who deeply cared for the children and took care of them as every child should be. Unfortunately for the children, she was to remarry and had decided to leave the orphanage with her children.

Rosa Carmichael became the next matron of the orphanage. She was the polar opposite of the first patron and soon came to gain a reputation as a tyrant. It has been speculated as to how she came into the position. Rumor had it that she had some influential friends in politics and that was how she came to be.

The children would come to live in fear of this woman. The tactics that she used to discipline them were horrendous. She would employ the use of the older boys to inflict justice upon the younger children. If a child misbehaved, oftentimes, their punishment consisted of being stood in a barrel of water up to their chests where they would remain for days. The children would be kept in the basement and the depiction of the young child in the pit was typically how she would treat the children. A child would eventually die under her care and the specifics on how the child died and to what happened to his body was never really known.

The town now having had enough of this woman, made an inquiry as to what was going on in the orphanage. Rosa would claim that the child died of natural causes and that they buried him somewhere on the property, but where, she couldn't exactly remember. The result of the inquiry was that of a $20 fine to Ms. Carmichael and that she had to leave town immediately.

The orphanage would soon close thereafter.

CHILDREN PLAYING

On the same night that Carol, Kim, Kat, and I had interviewed Joe Svehla at the Jennie Wade House, he had decided to take us over to the orphanage. No one from group had ever been there and we were all very excited to have the opportunity to go and see it. The museum/orphanage is across the street from the Jennie Wade House. We followed Joe over to the museum and stood behind him. He went to go unlock the door.

"Hmm, the key isn't working. I can't get the door unlocked!" Joe said, as he turned to look back at us.

"This has never happened before. I've never had any problem with this key." He tried again to get the door to unlock. Putting the key in, he grabbed the knob at the same time and tried to jiggle the door as he attempted to unlock it. He was unsuccessful—the door would not unlock.

"Alright, well, I will be right back. I am going to get the other keys from Bob. Stay here," he said and then turned and went back across the street to the museum shop for the Jennie Wade House.

I turned to look at Carol and the others and said, "That is interesting. Is the lock broken?" I stepped up close to the door and cupped my hands on the glass so that I could take a look inside the dark museum. Joe returned a few minutes later with other keys and stepped up to the door again.

"Let's see if these work," he said.

He put the key in the door and turned it slowly. The door unlocked and he pushed it open. We followed in behind him, one by one. He closed the door behind us and then went to turn on the lights. Was it possible that something was trying to keep us out? I believe it to be that something or someone at that particular moment did not want us to enter the building. Was it the spirit of a child being playful or something that was set on not letting us in?

He began to tell us the story of the orphanage and about Rosa Carmichael and how she treated the children. He then brought us over to the pit where the mannequin of the small child was. He turned on the audio tour and let us all listen as the boy told us his story. Joe then explained that the basement was the most active for paranormal activity and that was where they would take groups on the ghost tour. He then went and opened the basement door and we made our way into the basement.

The basement is sectioned into two rooms. There are wooden benches in the bigger room at the bottom of the steps. There is an open doorway that goes back into the smaller section. It gets much narrower as you step into that area. You have to go back and duck down under some pipes and then immediately off to the left is an opening in the wall where a crawl space is. Kat and I were instantly drawn to this area. It was as though something were calling out to us both. I felt compelled to follow her and see what it was that was drawing us to that area. Kat began to sense that there were children present in the basement and that there was a little boy in particular that she felt was there.

"Don't be afraid! Come out and see us," she beckoned as she motioned with her hands. We knelt down at the opening of the crawl space. It seemed that she had the sense that he was hiding there in the space.

"We aren't here to hurt you. We want to play! Please come out!" she said again.

"Yes, please come out and talk to us," I added.

"My name is Kat! Come out and play with us!"

"My name is Mark. Please come out."

I looked at Kat and had the strange sensation that others were present, too. We were not alone. Kat and I remained back there for several more minutes, hoping that the child would come and interact with us, but it didn't seem like it wanted to do so. We finally turned and joined the others in the main section of the basement.

Carol and Kim were sitting on one of the benches, and Joe was sitting up on the stairs near the door. We began chatting, and all of a sudden, we heard what sounded like children running across the floor directly above us! They ran from our right to our left directly overhead.

Carol's face lit up and her eyes went wide… "Did you hear that?" she asked.

"Yes, it sounded like children running," I replied.

"There are apartments above the museum with a stairwell directly above you," Joe stated plainly.

I paused and thought to myself that what I'd heard was not someone going up the stairs; there were too many footsteps and they were short fast strides across the floor—not the kind that you typically hear going up a set of steps, even if the person was running.

Joe had given us the opportunity to do an EVP session in the basement. It seemed to already be fairly active so were optimistic that we would be successful with a session. I decided to go and sit in the doorway that led back to the other section of the basement. I sat with my back facing that area, facing out towards the group in the main part of the basement. I let Kat and Carol lead the EVP session and I sat quietly.

"Is there anyone here that would like to speak to us tonight?" Carol asked aloud.

"Are you here? Please come and talk to us," Kat said.

"What are your names?" Carol asked.

"Do you like to play down here?" Kat asked.

Still sitting quietly, I slowly started to have the sensation that something was coming up behind me. I could feel cold wrapping up behind me, on the back of my neck and around my waist. It felt as though something was almost trying to hug me from behind.

"I have the feeling of something coming up behind me," I told the others.

"What does it feel like?" Carol asked.

"It feels like someone touching the back of my neck and around my waist," I replied.

"I think that someone is trying to get my attention," I added.

The feeling continued throughout the rest of the EVP session. It felt like a small child was running back and forth behind me. It would come up to me, touch me on the back, and then run away, back towards the back of the basement. I began to turn back to look into the basement, and every once in a while, I'd catch movement of a shadow. It was ducking in and out, but I could not really make out what it was. It was definitely playful and seemed inquisitive. I turned back to the group and again the rush of cold air came up and wrapped around me. I felt it all over my neck and back. There was definitely someone behind me.

From Carol's View

After visiting the Jennie Wade House, we walked across the street to the Soldiers Museum/Orphanage. As we approached the door, Joe put the key in the lock and the door wouldn't open. He tried several times, telling us that this has never happened to him before. After several more tries, he walked back across to the Jennie Wade House to get another set of keys. He came back over and after a couple of tries, the door opened. It struck me as very odd that this was the first time that the keys would not unlock the door. I had a strange feeling that something inside didn't want us to enter.

As you enter the museum, you see the gift shop and desk on your left. Right past that and to your right is a doorway. Joe showed us the exhibit of the "dungeon" that is located on the main level. As we were standing there listening to Joe and looking at the display, we heard a loud noise come from the main area by the front door. I looked, but didn't see anything there.

As you look down into a stone pit where young boys were kept and punished. He explained that after the battle, this orphanage was opened to care for the orphans of men killed in the battle. The first woman who was the headmistress was a kind person and cared for the children. After she left, she was replaced with a woman who was the exact opposite of her. This woman hated children and punished and tortured many who were staying there. She incorporated a few of the older children to help her with this.

Joe then started to lead us downstairs to the basement area. As he unlocked the basement door, he stood back. He said that as he turned the knob, the door was pulled out of his hand. We climbed down the narrow staircase to the basement. Joe talked about the children being lead down there and put in the hole and tortured. Out of over 100 children that originally were in the orphanage, only 10 were left after this headmistress left. Several of the boys were known to have fled to the Jennie Wade House across

103

the street where they felt safe. As we settled down on the benches, we all heard sounds of children running up above our heads. This went on for about a minute or so.

Our group then walked around the area and took pictures and EMF readings. After awhile, Joe turned off the lights and we began an EVP session. Joe sat on the staircase, Mark sat in the archway leading back to the dungeon, Kat sat on a bench in front of the stone wall, and Kim and I sat on a bench in front of Kat. I asked questions during the EVP session, Mark reported feeling heaviness behind him and seeing movements also.

Afterthoughts

It was a very interesting experience. In the short period of time that we were there, we had had some fairly significant occurrences. I, personally, had direct contact with someone, or something, in the basement when it was physically interacting with me during the course of the EVP session.

We were excited to hopefully have an opportunity to come back to do a formal investigation of the museum with our full team. It would only be a few months later in February of 2008 that we would return to complete a formal investigation of the Soldiers History Museum/Orphanage.

CCPRS FORMAL INVESTIGATION
FEBRUARY 16, 2008

It was day two of our weekend of investigations in Gettysburg and another cold and clear night as we gathered outside the front doors to the museum. Bob had pulled his vehicle up and we all began to unload. We knew from the beginning that our focus was going to be on the basement and that was where we had originally intended to concentrate our efforts. Tonight, we had our friend and colleague Robbin Van Pelt joining us for the investigation. Robbin has always been a valuable addition to any investigation. I have had the pleasure of working with her many times and knew that the Orphanage investigation was something that she should be a part of. Robbin has been investigating for many years and brings a lot of professional experience with her. She is an expert in photography and photographic analysis; her attention to detail and technique is something that has always been an added value to any CCPRS investigation that she has participated in.

We had decided that we were going to make the gift shop area our base and where the DVR system would be set up. It would prove to be an active night. We had just started setting up equipment and several teams had been deployed to start creating the floor maps and taking the base line readings, when a significant experience happened for several members of the team.

Only the Shadow Knows

Melissa, Mary, Kat, and Ken were working in the museum section of the building when Melissa first saw the apparition. It was a gray mass that was similar to a shadow person with no real definable features. It appeared at the end of a hallway and then shot to the right, out of view. In just a few minutes Mary, Ken, and Kat would also see the apparition in the hallway.

Mary would later write about the event in her investigative report:

"While I was mapping with Ken, I saw a gray shadow in the hallway going toward the area of cases of re-enactments in the museum. It literally darted down the hallway and turned right a few seconds later. Ken asked if I saw a gray shadow and I said yes. Ken and I, along with two other investigators, followed it until it disappeared. We all saw the same thing."

This photo shows the hallway located in The Soldiers Museum section where several investigators chased a shadowy figure.

There had not been very much activity reported in the museum area itself, but that night it seemed that there definitely was some activity. Bob and I had some discussion about the event and decided that we would put a DVR camera facing down the same hallway where the apparition had been seen. I had also decided to set up motion sensor that would shoot an IR (infra red) beam down the hallway. If anything broke the beam, an alarm would go off signaling to the team that something, or someone, was in the hallway.

The teams had completed the floor maps and taking the initial base readings. Bob and I had finished setting up the DVR system. We had placed a camera in the hallway of the museum and put the rest of the cameras in the basement.

One camera was in the main area, another shooting into the other section where the ITC device had been set up, and the final camera in the crawl space where the presence of a child had been felt during our previous visit.

The group was split into two teams. Isaac, Carol, Robbin, and I were in one team and Kat, Bob, Melissa, Ken, and Mary were in the other. Bob Michaels, our tour guide would hang out in the area of the DVR system, and later on, he joined my team for the ITC

session in the basement. My team was going to begin its investigation in the museum.

On this particular investigation some of the equipment being used played an important role in our ability to communicate with the spirits that reside in the orphanage. This would be my first time using a K2 EMF meter as an ITC device. We would use it in a way to receive yes or no answers from the spirits. We also were using a Cen-Tech thermo-coupling thermometer with a type K probe. This thermometer takes real time air temperature readings and displays it in tenths of a degree, i.e., 66.3 F. Bob also introduced his static-electric detector as another tool to be used during the investigation. Simply put, it detects static-electricity in the air and will light up and make a steady tone when it detects it.

We began our EVP session in the isle of the museum at the farthest wall, where the weapons were in display cases. Carol would begin the session as we stood in a circle at the end of the aisle.

An EVP Session

Carol asks, "Is there anyone here with us tonight? If there is someone here, could you… Okay, I see a light going on; is that a yes? I need one flash for yes and two for no."

The motion detector goes off. I turn to look to see if anyone or thing is in the hallway in the direction of the equipment. There is nothing to be seen.

Carol asks, "Can you give me one flash for yes and two for no?"

I am holding the K2 meter out in front of me. The meter is measuring EMF, but does not react as we had instructed it to.

The K2 meter has five LED lights across the top for measuring the EMF fields. It is used in ITC and EVP research by instructing the spirit to affect the field and manipulate the LED lights on the meter; one light for yes and two lights for no.

"Is there somebody with us tonight?" Carol asks. The meter remains the same.

"Did we scare you away?" she asks.

I turn and continue to look around in our general area to see if anything or anyone is near.

"Is there someone here with us, one for yes and two for no?" she asks aloud.

"Can you give us a sign that you're here?" The meter remains inactive.

"Are you associated with anything here in the museum?"

Isaac turns and takes another picture behind where we are standing.

"Do you wear a uniform that is here in the museum?" The meter does not respond.

"Can you come closer to us and signal that machine (referring to the hand held K2 meter)? Signal it once if the answer is yes and make it go twice if the answer is no."

The motion detector goes off again. Isaac then turns and takes a picture in the direction of the hallway.

"Are you afraid to talk to us? You can use us to gather all the energy you need to make the light go."

The meter begins to fluctuate as the first LED on the meter flashes off and on.

"Are you a man?" There is a pause. We remain quiet.

"Are you a child?" The meter does not respond.

"Are you a woman?" The meter remains inactive.

"Do you mind having people here tonight?"

Isaac turns and takes another picture in the general area we were standing.

"Is there any kind of message you would like to give us?" The quiet of our surroundings remains, as we stand waiting for a sign of a presence.

"Is there something vibrating?" Carol asks inquisitively as she looks about the room. "I hear vibration."

We all begin to look about to see what the cause of the vibration is.

"Is it the K2?" Carol asks.

"No, it's not the K2," I reply.

"Okay..." she says.

"Why don't we move farther down the hall into another section of the museum," I suggest.

"Lead the way," Carol answers.

We switch off with the meter and now Carol is holding it. It takes her a moment to get situated. The issue we were having with the meter at that time was that you had to hold a button down in order for the meter to stay on. We had not yet realized that you could use a coin to wedge into the device to keep the button depressed. We were still just learning how to use the meter at this point.

"That's better," Carol says.

"Are we ready to continue?" I ask.

"Okay," Carol replies.

"So, what do you guys think of this place so far?" I ask the group.

"This is awesome," Isaac replies.

"Back in here with some weapons, guns, look at the guns, do you use one of these guns? And there are swords too! Are one of these guns yours?" Carol asks as she looks at the weapons in the display case.

"It's interesting how this meter works. So far, though it doesn't seem to appear that we are having much success with it yet," I state to the group.

"We'd like to have you answer us. Use that small light, make that light flicker; if you want to say yes, flicker it once; if no, flicker it twice," Carol states. Would you like to talk to us? Is there something preventing you from talking to us? Were you at the Battle of Gettysburg?"

"It seems quiet," I reply.

"You were here at the Battle of Gettysburg?" Carol asks again.

"YES." (K2 indicated yes with one light) The meter responds to the question.

"Is your uniform blue?" The meter goes quiet again.

"Is your uniform gray or do you live here in Gettysburg? And now remember, we want one flash for yes and two flashes for no," Carol states. Do you understand? We have Isaac taking some digital pictures."

Isaac is taking pictures of the area documenting the display cases where we were working.

"I know you want to talk to us; you did it before." The meter fluctuates a little.

"Can you say *Hi* to us?" The meter flashes.

"Did you live here in the Orphanage?" The meter does not respond.

"Did you see any of the battle?" The meter remains quiet.

"Would you like us to go somewhere else in the building?" The meter flashes.

"Do you have someplace to show us?" The meter flashes again.

"Looks like we have some shells here, some cannon balls… were they loud?" The meter does not respond.

"Did a cannon ball hit your house?" It stays quiet. I look around again in the area behind where we were all standing.

"Are you wearing any medals on your shirt?" The meter is dark.

Isaac points to a picture in the display case. I come over and look at it with him.

"Do you know who General Lee is? Do you like General Lee?"

A knocking sound is heard in the distance; coming from somewhere behind us.

"Did anyone else hear that?" I ask.

"Yeah, I heard it, too." Robbin replies.

I look around and see if anyone from the other team has come into our area, but no one is found.

Carol asks, "Do you know who the president of the United States is? Is it George Washington?" No response from the meter.

"Is it John Adams? Is it Abraham Lincoln?" The meter stays dark.

"Do you not want to talk to us tonight?" The meter flashes.

"Are you too tired?" The meter flashes again, but does not give a definitive answer.

"I hear footsteps," Carol states.

"Yeah, where is it coming from?" I ask.

"They stopped," Carol says. "It sounded like footsteps on wood."

"Yeah, it did," I agreed.

We decided to make our way into the part of the museum where there were life-size mannequins depicting a scene by a creek. The representation is complete with a full-scale replica of a horse. (Which was a little disturbing in a very darkly lit environment.) There is a path through the scene; on both sides there are trees and shrubbery that reach all the way to the ceiling. It felt more like a jungle then something that would have been in Gettysburg.

We enter the hallway where the camera and motion detector are located. The motion detector begins to alarm as we break the beam. Immediately on the left of the hallway is a six-step stairway that goes down into the "Jungle scene."

"We're now entering the Gettysburg jungle!" I remark. "Oh, just got something right here!" I say, as the EMF fluctuates and the temperature drops. It happened very fast and almost immediately the readings returned to normal.

Carol says, "Are you following us down here? Were you walking down the steps with us?" Carol asks. "Do you think these things are funny? I think they're funny." Carol refers to the mannequins that are surrounding us on both sides of the path.

"Do you like looking at these little things or do they bring back memories?" The meter flashes and then goes dark.

"Can you make something move in here?" she asks. "Are you following us? You can walk with us; its okay. We're not here to hurt you; we're going over what looks like some kind of creek. If someone's over here, looks like down in the creek," she remarks.

I say, "Yes." The meter responded with a solid LED indicating the answer was yes.

Carol then jumps right into a line of questions hoping that the meter will continue to respond.

"Is that something you do? You were in the creek? Were you at a bridge? Sach's Bridge? Sach's Bridge, are you familiar with that bridge? How about Spangler Spring? There's got to be another bridge, right?" The meter remains dark through the questions.

She asks another series of questions. "This gentleman here is holding a flag. Do you recognize that flag? It looks to be a Confederate flag. Are you from the south? If you're in the service, do you have a specific job? Are you a soldier?" She pauses. "Its definitely cold in here."

"It's 74.8 degrees," I say as I look at the thermometer.

"It's colder than 74.8 degrees," she replies.

"It definitely feels colder than that," Robbin agrees.

"Okay, we're going to come back out this way," Carol says. "Are you going to follow us? You can come with us. Do you have a favorite place here in Gettysburg?" The meter does not respond.

"Are you married? Do you have children?" she asks. I think you're a little shy."

The sounds of footsteps are heard again.

"I hear the footsteps again," Carol says.

"Yeah, I heard them, too," I reply.

"Are you still with us or did you abandon us?" she asks. "I don't know, maybe we can have a man ask you questions. Would you prefer that?"

I take that as a cue to start asking questions.

"Do you want to talk to us?" I ask.

"If you want to talk to us, flash once for yes and for no, flash it twice. Are you here?"

The meter flashes, but again does not give a definitive answer.

"Are you here?" I ask again.

"Flash that once for yes, and twice for no." Do you understand?" Carol asks.

"62.5 degrees," I say to the group.

"Okay, we're going to walk a little bit further; do you want to come with us?" Carol says, as she begins to walk farther down the hall. We came to stop at a display depicting one of the battles at Gettysburg.

"The Battle of Gettysburg; were you here in July 1863?" Carol asks. "Do you live outside of Gettysburg?" The meter flashes.

"Did you camp out here in Gettysburg?" she asks. We hear a noise coming from behind us down the hall.

"Was that you?" Carol asks aloud. The LED's on the meter are lighting up and the meter spikes.

"Are you making the lights go on?" she asks. "Okay, I know you want to show us something; is that correct?"

The meter lights to answer "Yes."

"Okay; follow us," she replies.

"Looks like they're playing battle here with toy soldiers; do you play with toy soldiers?" she asks. The meter is quiet.

"We need to have some answers from you... Are you shy? You don't need to worry; we're not here to hurt you, and we just want to know more about you," she says.

"Do you feel safe here?" she asks.

"No." The meter replies by lighting two LED lights.

"Do you like living here?" she asks. Do you like to play games? Do you live upstairs here in the orphanage? Do you know what goes on down in the basement?" The meter flashes, but does not give a definitive answer.

"I know there's a way you can move this; you've done it before; just make it blink once."

The meter flashes.

"Do you understand?" she asks. "We've got a couple of different people playing with this meter; are you here with us?"

"Yes," the meter replies.

"Okay, is that fun?"

"Yes," the meter replies again.

"Do you want us to leave?"

"No," the meter lights in reply.

"Do you want us to stay here and keep you company?"

"Yes," it replies.

"How about if you run over, go over there, and make that machine beep? Go over there. We have a little red light on the machine over there; run in front of it. A red flashing light; run in front of it… That's all you have to do."

We wait to see if the motion sensor will go off. All is quiet…

An ITC Session

We ended our session and discussed our next session. We would do an ITC session in the basement in the back section of the basement. The K2 so far had been interesting, but I was curious to see it do more. We had some communication with something during the session, but it was not continuous. It seemed that whatever it was that was communicating with us would come and go.

It was time now to start our ITC session in the basement. Bob Michaels, our tour guide, had decided to join us during the session. He had been with my team on the previous night at the Jennie Wade house and I had extended the invitation to him to join us for the session. He has participated in many investigations at the orphanage and he had explained that he feels a connection with the children who reside there.

This photograph shows the staircase leading down into the basement where the children were taken to be punished.

The start time of our session was 9:24pm, and base EMF reading was .6, with the base temperature of 59.6 degrees.

"Carol, we'll let you lead it off and we'll take it like a free flow if anyone wants to join in," I say to her as the ITC device begins to sweep through the frequencies.

"Okay, good evening; is there anyone here that would like to contact us or speak to us?" she asks aloud. "Are there any children here?"

Click, click, click goes the ITC device as it sweeps through the AM frequencies.

"How old are you?"

A broken-up voice tries to come through on the device, but we cannot understand what it says.

"Can you speak louder, we can't hear you?" she asks. "What's your name? Do you like playing with toys?"

"The temperature has risen to 63.2 degrees," I announce to the group.

"Are you shy? You can come over and talk with us; we'd love to hear from you; is that okay? Are you frightened?" she asks in a series while trying to convey her sincerity in wanting to talk to the spirits of the orphanage.

"Children, this is Bob; you know me, and I'm down here quite often. I've brought some people with me tonight. You know I bring people down here. We try to contact you. And tonight, if you will speak to us, we will hear you. This is electronic equipment; you probably don't know much about that, but we can hear you tonight, if you want to talk to us," Bob explains. "So, Willie, are you here tonight?"

Click, click, click goes the device...

"Minnie, are you here?"

Inaudible chatter is heard; the device continues to sweep.

"Nate, are you here?"

"Tommy, are you here? You know there are so many of you children, that I don't always remember your names, but if somebody wants to let us know you're here—especially you, Willie; I know you like to let us know when you're around. Please say something." Bob pleads for the children to speak to us.

"66.5 degrees; its risen seven degrees so far..." I say to the group.

"Do you children remember Cathy?" Bob asks.

"Cathy." The device says.

"I heard Cathy," Carol states.

"Do you miss Cathy? I heard you say something... Maybe we can bring Cathy back over here if you miss her, but we need to know. Do you miss Cathy?" Bob asks.

"68 degrees…" I say as I keep my eyes focused on the thermometer which has now risen almost 10 degrees.

"I know sometimes you like to move the chain around. If you want to move the chain around tonight and show us that you're here, we would like that. We just want to visit with you for a little while. Come on, show us that you can move that chain."

The chain that hangs in front of the heater and boiler begins to sway a little.

"Can you move it a little more? Willie, I know you can move it. Who else can move it?" Bob asks.

"There's a ball on the bench; ask them if they want to move the ball." I suggest.

"Where is it?" Bob asks.

"It's on one of the benches down there," I say as I point to the other side of the basement.

"There's a ball on the bench; if you want to move that ball, you can move it. That's here for you. Last time I was down here, you showed us that you could move the chain. Do you want to show us again; we like that when you do it," Bob remarks.

"68.7 degrees…" I say as the temperature continues to rise.

"Does anybody want to tell us your name? We know you're here. Who is here tonight? Tell us your name."

The K2 meter begins to light up and the LED's light up to four lights and then waivers and falls back down.

"Hello Willie," Bob says.

"There's the K2…" I say and point at it. "Instruct the K2…" I say.

"Willie, if you're here, make the lights go to three lights for yes, that's it, keep doing it and four lights for no; can you show us no?" The K2 meter is lighting up and three LED's are lit… "That's it, one more; can you do it?" The meter jumps to four LED's and then falls back down to one.

"Can you pat Isaac on the shoulder?" I ask as I motion to him. "Are you still here? If you're still here, make it go to three lights… Come on, you can do it." I ask hoping to entice the spirits to respond favorably.

"Is there somebody else here with us? If you are, make it go to three lights. Who is here with us?" I ask.

"Tommy, if it is you, flash the yellow light…" Bob says.

"Amanda," The ITC device says in a clear male voice. It was so clear, it sounded as though it were right there in the room with us.

"Amanda? It doesn't sound like an Amanda," I remark.

"Woman?" Robbin asks.

"I know…" Carol remarks as she takes a picture.

"Is this Tommy? If it is, please flash the yellow light…" I ask.

The meter flashes yellow.

"Okay. What are some of the other names?" I ask.

"Matthew," Bob says.

"Matthew, flash the yellow light," I say.

The meter flashes yellow.

"Harry, Nate, we know you're here; let us know that you're here. Whatever children are here…" Bob says.

"71.5 degrees…" I announce.

"Tell us your name," Robbin says.

This is the basement in the Orphanage where children were taken to be tortured.

"Earlier this evening, some of us were being touched. You touched us; who was touching us? Who likes to touch us? Who pulled, who tugged? Was it Melissa's hair?" Bob asks.

"Kat's hair…" I reply. During the ITC session that Kat had been involved with, she had reported the sensation of someone pulling and tugging on her hair.

This photo is taken of an area in the orphanage known at The Pit. It is where children were put to be punished.

"Kat's hair; Willie, was that you?" Bob asks. "Blink the light if it was."

The meter flashes its LEDs.

"We know it was one of you," Bob remarks.

I put the thermometer on my lap and began to use the camcorder that I had nearby. I started recording and was scanning the room using the IR night shot on the camera. "Lost focus…" I remark.

The meter is flashing with three LEDs lit.

"Good, we see that… Was it a boy? Are you a boy who likes to tug women's hair?" Bob asks. You like to do that? Can you flash the light if you're a boy? I bet you do; it's kind of fun."

"You can touch us if you want, right? If you want to touch us, we'll let you," he remarks.

"72.3 degrees…" "It's risen 13 degrees since we started the session," I remark.

"Are you still down here with us? If you are, make the lights go up to yellow again. Make it flash up to yellow; are you still here? Yeah, can you do that again?" I ask.

The meter starts flashing yellow again.

"Good." Bob remarks.

"Why don't you run over this way, run past us?" I ask.

"Can you make the temp go back down? Can you make it cold for us? Can you make it go back down to 60 degrees?" Robbin asks.

"73.2 degrees…" I remark.

"Do you like it when we bring other children down into the cellar? Make the yellow light flash, if you do. You miss the children? We're going to be bringing some down pretty soon. They'll come and visit you. Would you like that? Can you blink the yellow light if you like it? Do you like other children down here?" Bob asks in a series of rapid questions.

The meter flashes yellow.

"Oh yeah… Very good… We saw that… A lot of children like you, too," Bob remarks.

"Do you play with the other children when they're here?" Robbin asks.

"Which is more fun to be with? Do you like to be with the boys? When the boys come down here? Make the red light come on if you like the boys."

The meter stays in the green and jumps up and down towards the yellow.

"Would you rather have girls? Make the red light come on for the girls. Would you like girls down here? Is that more fun?" Bob asks.

The meter spikes up into the red.

"Ahem. Thank you, we saw that; I'll remember that. Maybe it's Willie. Is that you, Willie? I think you like girls," Bob remarks.

"The top of my head is getting tickled," Carol remarks as she stays still.

"Are you tickling the top of Carol's head? If you are, make it go to red. Just once… You can do it," I say.

"Can you move the chain while you talk to us? Can you do that?" Bob asks. "I bet you can do that. There's probably a few of you children down here. Why doesn't somebody move the chain around, too? I'd like to see that. I haven't see that in awhile. I know you're good at it. Oh, I think you're playing games; I think you're going to move the chain around. I know you are. Just don't know when."

"Dropped to 71.1 degrees…" I say. "70…"

"Take it down to 60," Robbin says.

"69.8," I say. The temperature is now beginning to fall.

"How about 65? Can you take it down to 65?" Robbin asks.

"Cold, getting a cold spot behind my back…" I say.

"Right through here," Carol remarks as she motions with her hand to the area directly in front of where she is sitting.

"On my legs, too!" I exclaim. "69.5 degrees."

"Take it down to 65; see if you can do it!" Robbin says.

"68.9," I reply.

"Good job!" Robbin replies.

"Back up…" A voice is heard saying on one of the voice recorders during playback. At the time that it happened no one in the session had heard it.

"68.5 degrees… 67.9 degrees…" I remark.

"Take it to 65!" Robbin responds.

"67.5 degrees… 66.9 degrees…" I say as I watch the thermometer slowly falling.

A voice mumbles out from the ITC device, but no one can understand what it is saying.

"I didn't understand it, keep going," Carol replies as to what she heard on the ITC device.

"66.5 degrees," I reply.

"Come on!" Carol says.

"66.1 degrees…" I say.

"Almost there!" Bob says.

"65 almost…" Robbin remarks.

"Keep going…" Bob says.

"65.9 degrees…" I reply.

"Alright…" Bob says.

"Good job!" Robbin remarks.

"Three lights?" Bob asks.

"Good job, thanks guys!" Robbin says.

"The Tri Field hasn't moved at all. Got it on magnetic… 65.4 degrees… 65.3 degrees…" I reply.

"65 degrees…" Carol says.

"You're good!" Bob says.

"Okay, move it back up there, it's getting cold," Carol says.

"Take it back to where it's warm…" Robbin says.

"64.4 degrees…" "64.1 degrees…" I say.

"Okay, try going up; bring it back up into the 70s…" Robbin says.

"We're still falling; 63.7 degrees…" I say.

"Is it easier to touch us when it is cooler? Can you touch us now?" Bob asks.

"Yes," a voice says on the ITC device.

"Good," Bob says.

"Try a different frequency," Robbin states.

"63 degrees…" I say.

"Got to keep us warm now, hug us, give a big hug," Carol says.

"62.7 degrees…" I say.

"Can I ask a question?" Bob asks.

"Aha," Carol says.

"Children, I want to know…there's photographs upstairs; are any of you in those photographs that we look at. If you want to show me the red light on the meter like you've done, do that. Show me the red light. That means you're in the pictures upstairs, in the photographs. Are you in those photographs? I think you are; some of you boys I think are in there." Bob says.

"Do you like getting your pictures taken?" Robbin asks.

"61.7 degrees..." I say.

"We have some other pictures of you that people have taken, but the ones upstairs, you've probably seen those. Are you in those pictures? The old ones? Oh yeah, when the orphanage was in business and some children are playing games out there. That was fun, wasn't it?" Bob remarks.

"61.2 degrees..." I say.

"You're in the orphanage pictures? Are you in those photographs? Can you flick it to the red?" Robbin asks.

"60.9 degrees..." I say.

"You know upstairs, we have a picture of Alice. Alice, are you there?" Bob asks.

"60.7 degrees..." I say.

"Alice, are you here? You want to show us the red light if you're here. Fred, we don't ask for Fred too much. Is Fred here? Who's the other boy? Frank, are you here, Frank?" Bob asks.

"What was that?" I asked. "60.1 degrees... That's funny, they knew we were going until 10 pm; it's right where we started, right about where we started. 59.7 degrees..."

"You can tell time?" Carol asks.

"59.6 degrees..." I say. The temperature had risen to up over 70 degrees and then fell back down to where it was at the start of the session.

"Whew, that was awesome!" Carol remarks.

The clock had struck just about 10pm and the session had come to an end. It all happened in just thirty-six minutes. It was an intense session as we had direct responses from the ITC device, the K2 meter, and significant temperature changes during the event. I had never seen the temperature rise and fall so deliberately in the way that it had. I could explain that our presence being their increased the temperature of the room, but what could explain the temperature going all the way up and then coming back down to exactly the temperature it was when the session started? We had definitely made contact with the children in the orphanage. Their presence was made known to us.

The other investigative team had had their show of experiences, too. It was during the ITC session in the basement that several investigators had a physical interaction with the spirits. Bob, Kat, and Melissa all reported being touched in some way. Melissa even reported that something had hit her hard on the back of the head. She had come up from the session and was so emotionally charged that she broke down and then had to remove herself from the environment. It would take some time for her to calm down and she made it known that she would not go back down into the basement. She remained upstairs in the museum for the rest of the night, because of what had happened to her there. Kat had been running her own audio recording device along with the ITC device and had picked up quite a few EVPs of her own in direct response to her questions.

More Basement EVP

The following is an EVP transcript from a session conducted by Kat. These answers were imprinted on a standard digital audio recorder and not onto the ITC device. It seems that they were in direct communication with someone in the basement. The recording is quite remarkable to hear as the answers come to the questions.

Counter: 4:07:
"Are there any spirits or entities… that would like to speak with us?"
Answer: *Record the truth*

Counter: 9:03
"What is your name?"
Answer: *Mary*

Counter: 10:45
"Would you like to speak with us?"
Answer: *No*

Counter: 11:11
"Are you scared down here?"
Answer: *Yes*

Counter: 11:54
"Did you know Jennie Wade?"
Answer: *Yes*

Counter: 12:09
Answer: *Yes*

Counter: 12:31
"Did you live in Gettysburg?"
Answer: *Yes*

Counter: 15:01
"Do you go to school?"
Answer: *Yes*

Counter: 15:24
Answer: *Yes*

Counter: 15:42
"Is there a girl named Matilda?"
Answer: *Yes*

Counter: 15:58
"Is there a boy named Avery here?"
Answer: *Here (whisper)*

Counter: 16:23
Answer: *(Sounds like Jeffrey)*

Counter: 20:20
"Did you know any of the children in the orphanage?"
Answer: *Yes*

Counter: 20:26
"Is there a child behind me?"
Answer: *Yes*

Counter: 21:03
"Is there someone in front of me?"
Answer: *Yes*

Counter: 21:22
"Amy are you touching my hand?"
Answer: *No*

Counter: 22:36
"Did anybody try to hurt you?"
Answer: *Thank you (whisper)*

Counter: 23:05
"Were you ever allowed out of this basement?"
Answer: *No*

Counter: 27:15
"Do you know who Robert E. Lee is?"
Answer: *Robert E Lee (whisper)*

Counter: 32:16
"What do you like to eat?"
Answer: *(Male voice) Food*

Counter: 32:40
"Do you like chocolate?"
Answer: *(Male voice) Yes*

Counter: 33:02
"Do you like pumpkin pie, apple pie?"
Answer: *(Male voice) Pumpkin*

Counter: 34:20
"Are you making me cold?"
Answer: *Yes*

Counter: 34:23
"Do I have a little one on my lap?"
Answer: *Yes*

Counter: 38:18
"Pocket full of posies" (Melissa just said nursery rhyme)
Answer: *Here (whisper)*

Counter: 38:20
"Okay, let's try another one you might know…"
Answer: *Okay*

Counter: 38:57
"Don't want to sing for us much, huh?"
Answer: *"N" (male voice)*

Counter: 36:25
"Do you wonder what we are?"
Answer: *(Inaudible whisper, stairs creaking)*

Counter: 37:10
"What would you like to tell us; tell us now?"
Answer: *Home.*

Counter: 38:03
"Do you have a full belly?"
Answer: *What the…*

Counter: 39:27
"Come back; what would you like to talk about; please come back…"
Answer: *Quiet (whisper)*

Counter: 41:09
"Do you like dollies?"
Answer: *(Inaudible whisper)*

Counter: 46:36
"Do you want to pull on my braid again?"
Answer: *(Sigh)*

Counter: 49:19
Answer: *I am behind you (Woman's voice)*

Counter: 51:02
"Is there a mean lady here now; are you scared of her?"
Answer: *Yes*

Counter: 59:28
"Is there someone here named Charlie?"
Answer: *Yes*

Counter: 64:10
"Do you want me to leave, really?"
Answer: *No*

Group Session

The team finished the investigation that night with a group ITC/EVP session in the main room of the basement. We had used various types of EMF meters and had also used the static electric detector that Bob had brought to the investigation. The session lasted for forty-five minutes, and during that time, the children would come to play with us.

It was like a rush of energy would come into the room; everything would be quiet and then, all of a sudden, the meters would start to go off and the environment changed. I had decided to sit in the doorway with my back to the other part of the basement as I did before during the visit in November. It was almost immediately again that the spirits would come to play with me. I constantly had the feeling of someone running up behind me and putting their arms around me. The cold crept up around my neck and shoulders and would wrap up around me at the waist. It was a constant back and forth as though it really wanted to get by me and I was blocking its way.

We had captured a number of EVPs during this investigation. There was also a great controversy with a photograph that Melissa took. The photograph was down the hallway in the opposite direction from where the apparition had been seen. It was taken showing the DVR camera pointing at her. What made this picture a center of debate was that at the end of the hallway the image of a figure could be seen; a head and face, the outline of the body and then the shoes. The image was distorted and could

This photograph shows investigator, Robbin Van Pelt, in the Soldiers Museum. There is something located to the left of her. One of our investigators, Melissa, had taken the photo and noticed that there was something showing up that could not be explained. What do you think it is?
Courtesy of Melissa Daniels

not be easily identified as to who or what it was. Melissa had taken a second photo with Robbin in it in the same hallway; facing the same direction. This photograph too had something strange in it. Ultimately, after painstaking review and analysis it was revealed that it was in fact Bob, the tour guide. He had stepped into the frame of the shot just as the photograph was being taken. It had caused the visual distortion which made it difficult to tell who or what it was at first. The interesting thing is; that the second photo that had Robbin standing in it could not be explained. There is something peering over the side of Robbin; faint yet still in the darkness.

Is the orphanage haunted? I would have to say that with all of the experiences had by the investigative team and the evidence collected that it truly is. The activity there is intense and if you are not prepared for it, it can take you by surprise.

Carol Starr

ALONE IN THE BASEMENT

I was visiting Gettysburg on my own and ran into Joe Svehla from Ghostly Images. He was so kind and generous to allow me access to The Orphanage basement by myself. I was thrilled to be able to go down there alone for a period of time.

I walked into the Soldiers Museum/Orphanage around 4pm and met with the manager, Cindy Sherwood. She is extremely nice and was filled with information about the place. She told me to go over to the basement and let myself in. There were to be open another forty-five minutes or so.

I walked over to the landing and the door to the basement and undid the latch. I grabbed the door knob, turned it, and nothing happened. I did this a few times while looking around the door to see if there was another lock that I hadn't unlocked, but there wasn't. I tried the door again and, once again, it wouldn't budge. I went back over to Cindy to ask if I was doing something wrong or had missed a lock.

She came over with me and looked at the door and said, "No, that's the only lock." She took the door knob in her hand, turned it, and it came right open!

I just stared at her and shook my head. Maybe someone there didn't want me down there. I thanked her and she walked back to her desk in the museum. I walked through the door and flipped on the light switch which gave a little light down in the basement. Leaving the door open, I proceeded down the ancient steps. At the bottom of the steps is the first room. It has several wooden benches and some heating equipment in the one corner. In the far end of this room is a table that people, over time, have left toys for the children that had been living there after the battle. I saw a small teddy bear, some jacks, balls, and dolls. As my eyes were getting adjusted to the darkness, I heard a loud bang which made me jump. I realized that the door at the top of the steps was slammed shut. I didn't hear anyone up there and just assumed someone there wanted me all to themselves down in the basement.

As you walk from the first room, you go through a stone archway into another room. This room has some equipment on the right and there are chains strung up so visitors can't touch the heaters, etc. Further back into this room is an area where some of the poor orphans were taken by the cruel headmistress and tortured.

You can crawl back into the area to see where there are chains on the wall to restrain these poor children. I walked back into the front area and sat down to just take in the quiet of the place. I looked over to the chain that was strung from the wall to a pillar in front of the furnace and it started to move, at first just slightly back and forth, then finally up and down as if some small hands were picking it up.

I also started to see shadows darting from side to side in the back room as if someone was running back and forth, possibly wondering who this lone visitor was. I talked to them and told them I was there to visit and I hoped they didn't mind that.

I felt very calm and welcomed there and before I knew it my hour had passed. I made my way up the steps and thought for a second that the door might now open, but it did. I enjoyed my visit to the Orphanage and the children that still remain there.

CHAPTER 10

Mark Sarro

THE HALL OF PRESIDENTS

A Hall is Born

The Hall of Presidents wax museum sits on Baltimore Street; just a few doors down from the Soldier's History Museum (The Orphanage) and not far from Cemetery Ridge. The building was once a home and was built some time in 1920s. It wasn't until the 1950s that the house was turned into a museum; and before the house was built, another house once stood there that went back to the time of the Civil War.

The story goes that the woman who owned the house had lived there many years; raised a family there and became very reclusive over time. She died in the house and willed the house to her daughter in the hopes that she would keep it in the family; that would not be the case. She quickly sold the house within a few months of her mother's death. The person who bought the house would not keep it long; within a month of owning it, they too sold it. The person who then purchased the house decided to turn it into a museum, and thus the Hall of Presidents wax museum was born.

The Hall of Presidents where an angry old woman watches investigators.

CCPRS Formal Investigation
January 17, 2009

CCPRS was offered an opportunity to investigate the museum and this was something that was very special to us as we'd returned to Gettysburg almost a year after our Orphanage and Jennie Wade House investigations. We had to wait until the off season, because the museums were usually busy with history tours by day and ghost tours by night.

It was bitter cold and starting to snow when we arrived at the museum. Bob Michaels, our tour guide, greeted us and we all went into the museum together. The museum is laid out on two floors; on the first floor, are the life-size wax figures of the presidents separated out into five rooms with an average of eight presidents or so in each room, bleacher seating against one wall, and the display on the other.

There was something a bit creepy about all of those figures standing there—lifeless, but with eyes staring out into the room. Minimal lighting was available in each of the rooms as the fluorescent lighting that was at the feet of the presidents on the display was meant to enhance the effects. The light cast long shadows out from behind the presidents and only added more to the growing atmosphere that surrounded us.

I slowly made my way through each room as we toured the museum. I noticed that some of the figures caught my attention more than others; I don't know if it was their stares or simply the way that they were posed. The figure of Eisenhower was of particular interest because of the way that the he was positioned. He was on the floor level leaning up against the railing that separated the room and display, dressed in his military uniform. He was unimposing, but you couldn't help but be drawn to him.

The second floor of the museum had miniature figures of the first ladies in their various inauguration dresses. They stood side by side in glass display cases that lined each wall of the numerous rooms. On the street side of the museum was a room set up as Eisenhower's art studio with him sitting in front of a painting with a brush in hand and a palette sitting on his lap. The room next to the art room was a gallery of reproductions of his various works. I had not previously realized just how creative he was and how good his paintings really were.

The basement was an altogether different story. We had to exit the building and go around to the side of it to get into the basement, as there was no direct entrance from the first floor of the museum. The basement was full of figures that had been retired with various "parts" and pieces of figures on shelves and different places about the basement. There was one figure in particular that was of special interest. Bob had said that this figure would oftentimes be found moved or turned in a different direction. The figure would move by itself or some unseen force would move it.

Our tour of the basement was our last stop before we would begin the investigation, but here already an investigator would have his first experience.

Disoriented in the Basement

I was at the back part of the basement when Rob called out to me.

"Mark…" he called out.

"Yeah, what's up?" I replied as I walked over to him. He stood there with a puzzled look on his face.

"What's wrong?" I asked him.

"It's weird; I am having the same feeling that I did before…" Rob said.

"What do you mean? Are you feeling disoriented?" I asked.

"Yeah, it just came on suddenly," he remarked.

"Show me where it started," I stated.

Rob turned and headed back the way he came to the middle of the aisle on one side of the basement. I looked to see if there could have been something that might have caused the reaction. It was very common for someone to have a great physical reaction to high EMF fields. Upon inspection, I did not see anything obvious that could have been the cause of it. Explaining to him that it would pass and that it could take some time, I reiterated to him that the sensation would go away. I too have these types of experiences and often it leaves me feeling out of sorts for a little while.

The team finished the tour and we made our way back up to the first floor. It was now time to start the investigation. We began by splitting up into two teams and proceeded to make floor maps and take base readings of the museum. For CCPRS, this is essential in order for us to better understand the environment that we are in and what it is that is around us. It forces us to gain an intimate knowledge of our surroundings and helps to us stay aware of the naturally occurring things that may be misinterpreted as paranormal.

It became obvious that something was present in the museum. The challenge is that when a place lies dormant with no one interacting with the environment, the place can settle down. We had been the first group of people to be in there in some time. Despite the fact that there might have been a high amount of paranormal activity; it still could be quiet and less active because of its dormant state.

The Paranormal Puck

CCPRS is always looking for new tools to use on investigations; whether it's an electronic device or simply a new method or technique. The Paranormal Puck is something that has added so much value to CCPRS in its information and data gathering as well as technique. The device was introduced to the group by Bob, my good friend and colleague. He has always stayed on the edge of the research and found the device and purchased it.

So, what is it? It is a device that has a collection of sensors that pick up various environmental information; radio frequency, temperature, humidity, AC EMF and natural EMF. The device connects to a computer via USB and interfaces with the custom software that was designed to collect the data. But what makes this device so interesting is that it then interprets the data into words and then will "speak" using the text-to-speech software built into it. It has a 2,500-word vocabulary that is based on some of the

most common words used in the English dictionary. It also includes proper names.

There is no algorithm that controls how the words are selected. There is a one-to-one relationship of the word to the readings that the device picks up. CCPRS has adopted it into its ITC research study, but it really is much more than that. It is not meant to speak in

One of CCPRS' investigators, Rob Devitis, preparing maps prior to the investigation.

sentences or even specific phrases, but we have found that it's all about the pattern or repetition of the words being said. The software has an interface that allows you to input questions into it. For example: I may ask, "What is your name?" And then the device will respond. There are several intervals that you can set for how long the device has to respond (i.e., 3 seconds, 5 seconds, 10 seconds, 15 seconds, 25 seconds, 45 seconds, 60 seconds and constant mode). It also stores all of the data into a spread sheet with a time stamp on every entry.

One of the ways that we use it is during a group session is that I will input the questions being asked by a member of the group directly into the interface. By doing so, we automatically have a transcript of everything that was asked, along with all of the data that the puck gathered. It has proven to be a remarkable tool, and in some ways, it has provided instant validation of the things that come through on the ITC device, because the two devices will begin to say the same things!

If you are curious to hear the device in action and in real time come and visit my radio show: *Voices Carry Radio* on Para-X. The show focuses on ITC research and every week we do live ITC sessions with the ITC device, Paranormal Puck and other tools. Go to: www.para-x.com for more information.

ITC Group Session 1:
The Presidents Room 2

I had completed a quick walk through with Mary and Dinah to determine where we should set up to do our first ITC and Paranormal Puck session.

Rob would write about an experience he had during the walkthrough in his investigative report:

"Before the group session, Mark, Mary, and I walked through. At 7:20pm, I experienced a touch on my right knee while in President's Room 2, next to the Buchanan statue."

We had set up the device along the top row of bleachers in the room. This was the room that had the depiction of Abraham Lincoln sitting at his desk off to the far side of the room from where we were sitting. We'd decided to start with the Paranormal Puck. I sat facing the laptop with Robbin sitting back to my left, then Dinah and Mary on the first row of seats, Rob sat up on the same level as the devices with Isaac sitting next to him, and Carol at the end sitting on the same level that I was.

I'd set the interval for the Puck at sixty seconds from the time that the question was asked. I liked to give it time to respond and see what patterns or repetition of words would develop. Dinah had also decided to use her pendulum in conjunction with the ITC device. She has developed a strong connection to it and has felt that the responses she gets to be genuine.

The following is a combination of the transcripts from Mary's reports as well as the Paranormal Puck Logs.

Mary asks: "Are there any spirits with us?"

The Puck would respond in its male computerized voice: "Stand enough recuse army cover human those clock students discovered Sandy iron Mandy seven Nancy tablet cross lay song cord yell. One scan beast strange wife divided"

The words appear random as they translate the environmental readings into these words, but is it possible that it did answer the question? *Army, Sandy, Mandy, seven, Nancy and Wife...* Could these be the answer? The repetition of the words and what we are looking for? Oftentimes, we will ask the same question several times. I believe that if there is an intelligent spirit present, it has to learn how to communicate through the device. Essentially, it has to manipulate

CCPRS investigators, Rob Devitis and Mary Gasparo collecting evidence during a recent investigation in the Hall of Presidents.

the environment in such a way that it will cause specific words to trigger. Or is it simply PK (Psycho kinesis), subconscious energy manifesting from those participating in the session? Let us continue to see how it develops...

Robbin asks: "When the students come through, do you see them?"

The Puck responds: "Control point brought. Minute laugh blind determine mass cried intention travel Paula leader became Don Mandy nerd soldiers beautiful Beth gun female rust we park"

Paula, Don, Mandy, soldiers, Beth and female... More names coming through, but Mandy has repeated and soldiers could be taking the place of the word army.

The Pendulum responds "No."

The pendulum is another ITC device that is used quite frequently by investigators and those of the more sensitive persuasion. It reacts in a very similar fashion to a pair of dowsing rods or even a talking board at its most elementary level. It answers in the simplest form—yes or no—and sometimes, if it doesn't react in one form or another, it could be interpreted as unsure or maybe.

Mary asks: "Is there a message you want to give?"

The Puck says: "Got before base surge need 7 done m anger town. Marry tip medicine. Paul Monica Providence movie home study feel tablet m metal mommy"

7, anger, Marry, Paul, Monica and mommy are worth notating. Anger more specifically could be part of, if not the answer, to the question asked. Mary had focused in on anger and Marry because of an experience that she had earlier while on the second floor.

Mary asks: "Are you the woman I saw upstairs?"

The Pendulum responds: "Yes."

The pendulum responded with a strong yes, further confirming for Mary that the woman that she had a vision of while on the second floor during the EVP session that Rob and I joined her on.

The Puck says: "Win sacred pattern between hour wait nerd cross wisdom goodbye. Kill call truck anger while Jupiter control learn recuse. Disaster melody head monitor we'll divided."

Anger is repeated again. The repetition of this word could be it trying to communicate in a very limited scope. Mary picked up on this and then decided on her next question.

Mary asks: "Why are you angry?"

The Puck says: "Unclear company no Sandy Malice dollar lemon agreed channeling drink female rather measure quill oil yield blanket malice solution hour tag matrix capital check ground table."

Unclear, company, Sandy, Malice… It spoke *malice* twice, but the first word in response was *unclear*. Was it "unclear" as to why it was angry? Maybe it couldn't fully express what it truly wanted to say.

Rob asks: "Is it okay we are here now?"

The Pendulum says: "Yes."

The pendulum swung to a resounding yes as it responded to Rob's question. The puck on the other hand would give its answer in cryptic fashion; forcing us to filter through the response to find the answer to the question.

The Puck says: "Mission workers. Go ahead nine weather vern mop pose brought spoon we this wife herd angry cave + cannon medicine page small. Halt funeral starve boy."

It did not seem to give us an answer to the question. I believe that, at times, it may still be trying to answer a previous question or learning how to manipulate the words so that it can communicate. The challenge lies in determining the difference between a potentially intelligent spirit or simply an active environment that is causing the words to trigger.

Robbin listened to the response and felt that it was still giving responses to the question, "Why are you angry?"

Robbin asks: "Are you angry with the workers?"

The Pendulum says: "Yes" then "No."

The pendulum quickly answered yes, but then suddenly turned to no.

The Puck says: "Mass Ed clouded work strength feel moment Ron snow enjoy shaken she enjoy raised deplete dock clouded Nancy divided 7 interrupt horse sign $ thus grand deal."

Clouded, snow, enjoy… It mentions *clouded* and *enjoy* several times. Since the device is measuring the environment, it seems that it may be sensitive to weather conditions. It was snowing at the time of the investigation and it is very possible that it was picking up on that.

Robbin realized this and decided on her next question.

Robbin asks: "Are you enjoying the snow?"

The Pendulum says: "No."

The Puck says: "Killed monument initial fact think sold yield vapor both clouded wild prepared father clear nine up thing. Husband grandmother kitty important. Fun turnover under."

It did not seem to have an answer; randomly it spoke as it measured the changes in the environment.

Robbin asks: "Are you cloudy about why you are here?"

The Puck says: "Verb mommy at beach release dance remain designate Karen kiss hallow brother did had knew mistress America tone silent give themselves measure restore Monica important."

The first session in the Presidents Room 2 was a short one. We had to stop because Carol was not well. In the session though, we realized the effect that the heating system was having on the environment as far as EMF fields were concerned. When the heat would come on, there would be a spike in the EMF field that would slowly subside. We had observed this phenomenon throughout the session. It was obvious though that something was trying to communicate with us despite the false readings created by the heating system on the EMF meters.

It is standard as part of our investigative reports for each investigator to write about their own personal experiences and make their own conclusion based on

Investigators, Rob Devitis and Issac Davis during the investigation of the Hall of Presidents.

what was experienced. When it comes time to present the evidence to the client, we take the collection of investigative reports and combine them together. It is an interesting way to see how the investigation was experienced from the point of view of each of the investigators. Here now I present several investigators reports verbatim to show it from exactly their points of view.

Dinah would write about the investigation and experience as a whole:

"My perceptions began some time before the actual investigation began as I drove into Gettysburg along Route 30—coming from the east to the west. As I got to the cross street at Fourth Street, my head began to swim. My equilibrium was greatly reduced. I feel this in a less drastic way, when I am being personally connected to paranormal activity. This method of identification began for me approximately two years prior while being mentored by psychic Laurie Hull during an investigation in Cape May, New Jersey. The top of my head, from my eyes up, will develop a dizzying sensation.

But this time, it was dramatic. It was so intense that I had to call out to my guides to throw up shields to take away the phenomenon. I was surprised and a bit scared because this had happened while I was driving. Seconds more and it would have been necessary to pull the car off the road. My guides did, indeed come to the rescue, and my dizzy feelings dissipated. This happened twice within a four block spacing until I finally implored the guides to keep my shields up at all times while I was driving a car.

A wax figure of President Lincoln in the Hall of Presidents.

There were no more impressions until the investigation began at the Hall of Presidents that evening. I found the location to be less active for me than other places I'd investigated (Eastern State Penitentiary, York Little Theater, Mark's haunted home), but the evening still had some learning experiences.

This was a location that provided first-hand understanding of EMF and its relationship to electrical equipment. The heating system routinely came on and went off all night long and we found that every time the heat came on, EMF spiked very high. Robbin did conduct one temperature experiment to show that there were times that the EMF readings were accurately showing possible paranormal activity, but knowing the high concentration of electrical interference made it difficult to determine accuracy.

At the Hall, I conducted several pendulum exercises and results were interesting, confirming an angry woman in the building, first sensed by Mary.

I believe, based on my own experiences and by witnessing experiences of other investigators, that there is paranormal activity of a mild nature at the Hall of Presidents. I believe that the spirits (in general) felt honored to be remembered in such a fashion and that the woman who seems to reside there (historically shown to live there at one time) may be more understanding of events now that we've had the opportunity to interact with her.

Upon reviewing my audio evidence, I found that, during a conversation with Mary in the lobby, there was the sound of children laughing on the cassette from my analog recorder.

Of special interest to me as an animal communicator for the group (and to my delight), I was put in touch with a dog belonging to the Calvin Coolidge family displayed at the side of a painting of First Lady Grace Coolidge on the second floor. I was first tipped off by EMF levels rising by her figure in the display case where prior base readings had shown zero activity. It was then that the dog popped into my mind. I saw it running and playing on the White House lawn. The important image of "outside" being important was pushed hard into my thoughts.

Later, I would discover that the Coolidges did indeed have such a dog who so loved the outdoors that it took quite some time to acclimate him to the White House rules. The dog's name was Rob Roy and was a sheep-herding dog from Wisconsin. (It's no wonder he didn't like being cooped up in the White House!) Rob Roy died in 1928.

Also after the investigation, I made an attempt to talk to the deceased dog through my animal communications ability. Almost immediately, I got the impression of Rob Roy crouching down with his front legs, as though ready to pounce. He was in a field of green grass and tall yellow and white flowers.

"I saw you that night," he said to me. "Thank you for calling me beautiful. That man with you was not so nice. I do not have mange."

One of the other investigators had not been impressed with the dog shown in the painting and told me that he thought that the dog had mange. I'd reprimanded him for such a statement. This was a beautiful dog.

The dog continued to tell me: "I loved my time with them [Coolidges] and I am with them again—though now I stay in the fields—I love the fields. I am well, but I will not be back. I will stay here. I am happy here."

Rob Roy ended with, "I was the best White House dog." And I was inclined to agree.

I believe that the dog, Rob Roy, came because of my personal connections to animals and the desires I felt to know him better. I have found, at least for animal spirits, that they can be summoned—and though they don't always come as requested, sometimes their interest is peaked and they do indeed connect. Rob Roy connected."

(Learn more about Rob Roy in Dinah's book, *Go To Hell: Ghosts, Pets, and Mysteries*, scheduled for release in Fall 2010.)

Mary would also tell of her experiences and the investigation as a whole:

"This is an old building and the floor boards make so much noise that it interferes with the audio. When we did a walkthrough, I didn't pick up anything unusual on the first floor. However, when I went up to the second floor, where we passed through the rooms with the First Lady miniatures, the hair on my left arm stood up. In the past, this is usually an indication that something is about to occur. As I went into the room with President Eisenhower painting, the feeling became stronger on my arm. So, I closed my eyes and had a quick glimpse of an older woman who was in a very angry state. As I went into the room with the paintings, the feeling subsided.

[Note: I was not familiar with the history of the building. So I asked Bob Michaels if this was someone's house at one time. He told me that it was until 1955, and then it was sold. He asked me if I had a reason for asking. I told him that when I was in the room with the President painting, I experienced a vision of an angry old woman. He validated my experience by telling me that a medium that was there in a prior investigation who had experienced the same thing in that very place! She died in the house and the daughter sold the house much to her dismay. This woman wanted the house to stay in the family. I believe that this is why the old woman may be in an angry state.]

Going into the basement, Rob was experiencing light-headedness and complained of being dizzy. I immediately went over to him to make sure he was okay. After I realized he was fine, I turned around to walk away and suddenly, in that very moment, I saw a shadow dart across the wall, near the opening of the basement. As far as I know, no one else saw what I saw.

Isaac and I mapped out the first floor and didn't notice anything to be unusual at that time.

Mark, Dinah, and I did a quick walkthrough to determine the best spot to do an ITC/Puck session. We agreed on the Presidents Room 2.

We started our first EVP, video, and photo rotation. Mark, Rob, and I started upstairs. Dinah, Carol, Robbin, and Isaac were on the first floor. While going through the rooms with the First Ladies miniatures, I didn't notice anything to be unusual. Rob, on the other hand,

A wax figure of President Eisenhower in the Hall of Presidents.

experienced another episode of dizziness and light-headedness. In the room with President Eisenhower, Rob experienced a feeling on his neck. I did not see the older woman, but had experienced the sensation of extreme anger.

In the room with the paintings, we did a vigil with the lights out. Mark and I heard some ticking, but I felt it was from the radiator or vents from the heat turning on. When we were leaving the room, we had heard a thump. I thought it was from the ceiling, but Mark and Rob felt it from the floor. So, I don't know if I could conclude as to whether it was sign of paranormal activity or merely the building shifting from the floor boards. But I will say this; it didn't sound like the noise the floor boards were making.

During the Puck session (In Presidents Room 2) there were temperature changes and high EMF spikes. Some of those changes were proven to be from the heater turning on. This was a very interesting session, because it validated what I felt and saw upstairs. During the course of the puck words, the name Mary came up quite a few times, followed by the word anger. I asked Mark to ask Bob Michaels (the tour guide) what the older woman's name was. He told us the name of the woman was Mary! Also I asked how many spirits where with us and we got the number 7. I looked around and counted seven president wax figures. Carol was feeling sick, so we ended the puck session. Dinah was using her pendulum throughout this session and was getting responses that were correlating with the puck.

After a short break, we stayed in President Room 2 and continued with the ITC session without Carol. We had Bob Michaels join us at that time. Mary came through on the ITC device. The questions that were being asked were mostly centered on Mary and her husband. It seems as though that she was not happy about the renovation being currently done on the front porch.

We brought the ITC/Puck equipment upstairs and then started another rotation.

Mark, Rob, and I did an EVP, video, and photo rotation on the first floor. Nothing unusual occurred, other than we made note going through the President Room 2 that the temperature had gone back up into the 60s. The temperatures during the ITC session in that room were much lower.

While we were in the President Room 3, Mark and I heard a noise that sounded like a man gasping. I noted that Bob Michaels was outside at the time. Rob did not hear the sound, but fortunately, I did capture it on my audio recorder. There was a photo that Rob took while in the President Room 3 that had an unexplainable form in it that will need to be further evaluated. Mark then heard something again which Rob and I did not initially hear. I believe though, upon further review of my audio recording, that I may have picked up the voice of a small child at the time that Mark heard the sound.

We regrouped and did a final ITC/Puck session on the second floor in the Eisenhower art gallery. The name Mary continued to come up during the session, but this time, it appeared that it may have in fact been a message directly related to me. The name Justin had also come up several times. The group asked if I knew anyone with the name of Justin and I replied that in fact it was the name of my Godchild. We also heard the name Bob several times throughout the session. I need to review the logs further to determine if there is any connection or message relating to that name. The session made a bizarre turn and the word feet kept coming up in various combination of words. The line of questioning then changed to try and see if there was anything to the repetition of this word. Towards the end of the session Rob broke into a laughing fit that seemed uncontrollable. Right before he started the outburst, you can hear heavy breathing on my audio recording. It was not Rob or any other member of the group. It sounded as though as if it were right on top of the recorder.

We then started packing up the gear, but had decided to go spend the remaining time that we had with a quick EVP session in the basement. We decided not to bring the ITC/Puck equipment on this last rotation but to do a standard EVP session with our analog and digital voice recorders. I did have an equipment failure with my camera and digital voice recorder. At various times during the session, I had a full battery drain three times on the digital audio recorder and two times on the camera."

Mary offers her final thoughts based on the experiences had during the investigation:

"I do believe that there is paranormal activity in the Hall of Presidents. It could be because no one has been in there for awhile, and if we came back [as I explained earlier] in a couple of days, that we may have an increase in paranormal activity within the museum. However, I do believe that the spirit of an angry old woman, "Mary," is there and still holding onto the bad feelings of her house being sold off by her daughter. It also appears that she is unhappy with the renovations that are underway on the front porch, along with the visitors that come and go in the house unannounced. (Or at least as she may perceive it.)

When we did the session as a group on the second floor, there were some things that came through that had nothing to do with the house or Gettysburg. An interesting note is that, at one point during the session, the question "Are you from another dimension?" was asked using the Paranormal Puck. The response that followed this question included the words "stars" and "portal." The Mary/Justin responses during that final group session is something that I would like to pursue further in the recordings, as well as the things that heard beyond the Puck or ITC device as they are personally important.

I am quite concerned that Rob lost control of himself during that final ITC session. I feel something may have taken him over, if only but for a brief moment. I feel that stronger grounding needs to be practiced at the start of the investigation so that we may be better protected against the possibility of anything negative happening."

There were some profound experiences reported by members of the investigative team that night—Rob with his physical reaction to the environment as well as being touched, Mary with her sense impression of the woman who was present in the museum, Dinah with her guides communicating to her via the pendulum and the animal communication that she had through the picture of the dog. Sounds and voices were heard, EVPs were captured and it seemed that at times during the night, we were in direct communication with the spirits of the building. They were not happy at times and had made their presence known.

I felt that the building itself had a lot of residual energies from the history of all that had gone on there. The Presidential wax figures themselves had a history, as some of them had come from other museums and, in a way, had their own stories to tell. The building lies dormant for many months during the off season and the spirits have nowhere to go and no one to communicate with. We had been the first people to spend time inside the building since the previous season had ended.

I too seemed have been effected in some way by something on the second floor during the final group ITC/Puck session. I had a hard time concentrating on the words, as though something was distracting me mentally and clouding my judgment. When Rob had had the outburst, it was sudden and unexpected. It was as though something had taken a grip on him and would not let him go. It passed, but at that point, it seemed that it had

succeeded in its purpose of disrupting the session and not giving us the answers that we were in search of.

Mary, the angered spirit who spent many years of her life in that house, was still there disapproving of all that went on—unsure of why or how it was that her home had come to be the way that it was; stranger upon stranger entering her home and wandering about her rooms. Did she even recognize her home? Was she struck with confusion which added to the anger? She struggled to understand her environment, yet she knew that she belonged there and that it was her home.

CCPRS was given a special opportunity, only being one of a very small number of paranormal groups given the opportunity to investigate and experience the Hall of Presidents wax museum. I take from the experience knowing that something was there, at times hidden, but still there making its presence known throughout the building. I encourage you to visit the Hall of Presidents for yourself and experience a very special part of Gettysburg.

For more information:

Hall of Presidents
789 Baltimore Street
Gettysburg, PA
717-334-5717

AFTERWARDS

We have now visited the sites and scenes of Gettysburg, yet there is still so much more to experience and see. The spirits have been playful, curious, and sometimes unsure. We have talked to them and they have given to us their story, as best that they could. We have looked at the research and gone deep inside the investigations to experience it through the eyes of the investigator.

The experiences are here waiting to be had and dare those to come and experience it for themselves. Go and visit these places; learn the history; experience the past and take from it all that it has to offer. We cannot fear it, but must learn from it.

This book is finished, but the research and study continues on long hereafter. We must continue to search for the answers and try and find the truths behind what happened to all those that came to Gettysburg... and stayed behind...

Glossary

Air Probe Thermometer
A thermometer with an external probe that is capable of taking instant measurements of the air temperature.

Anomalous field
A field that cannot be explained or ruled out by various possibilities, that can be a representation of spirit or paranormal energy present.

Apparition
A transparent form of a human or animal, a spirit.

Artificial field
A field that is caused by electrical outlets, appliances, etc.

Aural Enhancer
A listening device that enhances or amplifies audio signals. i.e., Orbitor Bionic Ear.

Automatic writing
The act of a spirit guiding a human agent in writing a message that is brought through by the spirit.

Base readings
The readings taken at the start of an investigation and are used as a means of comparing other readings taken later during the course of the investigation.

Demonic Haunting
A haunting that is caused by an inhuman or subhuman energy or spirit.

Dowsing Rods
A pair of L-shaped rods or a single Y-shaped rod, used to detect the presence of what the person using them is trying to find.

Electro-static generator

A device that electrically charges the air often used in paranormal investigations/research as a means to contribute to the materialization of paranormal or spiritual energy.

ELF

Extremely Low Frequency.

ELF Meter/EMF Meter

A device that measures electric and magnetic fields.

EMF

Electro Magnetic Field.

EVP

Electronic Voice Phenomena. The act of catching disembodied voices or imprints of paranormal events onto audio recording devices.

False positive

Something that is being interpreted as paranormal within a picture or video and is, in fact, a natural occurrence or defect of the equipment used.

Frank's Box

An ITC device created by inventor Frank Sumption. This device is custom built using various parts from HAM and shortwave radios.

Camera

A 35mm film camera connected with a motion detector that is housed in a weather proof container and takes a picture when movement is detected. Made by Silver Creek Industries.

Geiger Counter
A device that measures gamma and x-ray radiation.

InfraRed
An invisible band of radiation at the lower end of the visible light spectrum. With wavelengths from 750 nm to 1 mm, infrared starts at the end of the microwave spectrum and ends at the beginning of visible light. Infrared transmission typically requires an unobstructed line of sight between transmitter and receiver. Widely used in most audio and video remote controls, infrared transmission is also used for wireless connections between computer devices and a variety of detectors.

Intelligent haunting
A haunting of a spirit or other entity that has the ability to interact with the living and do things that can make its presence known.

ITC
Instrumental Trans Communication. The means of communicating with spirits by way of a device, i.e., digital voice recorder, Video Feedback, ITC Device, EVP, Talking Boards, Pendulums.

ITC Device
An electronic device created with modified radios and other electronic devices that is used for real time communication with the spirit world.

Milli-gauss
Unit of measurement, measures in 1000th of a gauss and is named for the famous German mathematician, Karl Gauss.

Orbs
Anomalous spherical shapes that appear on video and still photography.

Pendulum
A pointed item that is hung on the end of a string or chain and is used as a means of contacting spirits. An individual will hold the item and let it hang from the finger tips. The individual will ask questions aloud and the pendulum answers by moving.

Poltergeist haunting

A haunting that has two sides, but same kinds of activity in common. Violent outbursts of activity with doors and windows slamming shut, items being thrown across a room and things being knocked off of surfaces. Poltergeist hauntings are usually focused around a specific individual who resides or works at the location of the activity reported, and, in some cases, when the person is not present at the location, activity does not occur. A poltergeist haunting may be the cause of a human agent or spirit/energy that may be present at the location.

Portal

An opening in the realm of the paranormal that is a gateway between one dimension and the next. A passageway for spirits to come and go through. See also Vortex.

Residual haunting

A haunting that is an imprint of an event or person that plays itself out like a loop until the energy that causes it has burned itself out.

Scrying

The act of eliciting information with the use of a pendulum from spirits.

Sleep Seizures

Also known as a Focal Seizure, this is in between sleep and consciousness when the mind is awake and conscious but the body is still asleep. The sensation of a buzzing or electric sound felt or heard, the body is paralyzed, auditory hallucinations and sometimes visual hallucinations can occur.

Strobe Light

This is a light that is set on a variable timer that flashes in quick successions and is controlled by a dial that can speed up or slow down the rate at which the light flashes.

Table Tipping

A form of spirit communication, the act of a table being used as a form of contact. Individuals will sit around a table and lightly place there fingertips on the edge of the table and elicit contact with a spirit. The Spirit will respond by "tipping" or moving the table.

Talking Boards

A board used as a means of communicating with a spirit. Also known as a Quija Board.

Tone Generator

A device used to produce specific audio frequencies. This kind of device is often used as a test gauge for calibrating and troubleshooting certain types of audio equipment.

Video Feedback Loop

This is type of visual distortion that is produced when a video camera is connected directly into a television and pointed back directly into the television, thus causing a loop that feedbacks into itself.

Vortex

A place or situation regarded as drawing into its center all that surrounds it.

White Noise

A random noise signal that has the same sound energy level at all frequencies.

EQUIPMENT EXPLANATIONS

In this section, the Chester County Paranormal Research Society looks at the application and benefits of equipment used on investigations with greater detail. The equipment used for an investigation plays a vital role in the ability to collect objective evidence and helps to determine what *is* and *is not* paranormal activity. But a key point to be made here is: the investigator is the most important tool on any investigation. With that said, let us now take a look at the main pieces of equipment used during an investigation...

The Geiger Counter

The Geiger counter is device that measures radiation. A "Geiger counter" usually contains a metal tube with a thin metal wire along its middle. The space in between them is sealed off and filled with a suitable gas and with the wire at about +1000 volts relative to the tube.

An ion or electron penetrating the tube (or an electron knocked out of the wall by X-rays or gamma rays) tears electrons off atoms in the gas. Because of the high positive voltage of the central wire, those electrons are then attracted to it. They gain energy that collide with atoms and release more electrons, until the process snowballs into an "avalanche", producing an easily detectable pulse of current. With a suitable filling gas, the flow of electricity stops by itself, or else the electrical circuitry can help stop it.

The instrument was called a "counter" because every particle passing it produced an identical pulse, allowing particles to be counted, usually electronically. But it did not tell anything about their identity or energy, except that they must have sufficient energy to penetrate the walls of the counter.

The Geiger counter is used in paranormal research to measure the background radiation at a location. The working theory in this field is that paranormal activity can effect the background radiation. In some cases, it will increase the radiation levels and in other cases it will decrease the levels.

Digital and 35mm Film Cameras

The camera is an imperative piece of equipment that enabled us to gather objective evidence during a case. Some of the best evidence presented from cases of paranormal activity over the years has been because of photographs taken. If you own your own digital camera or 35mm film camera, you need to be fully aware of what the cameras abilities and limitations are. Digital cameras have been at the center of great debate in the field of paranormal research over the years.

The earlier incarnations of digital cameras were full of inherent problems and notorious for creating "false positive" pictures. A "false positive" picture is a picture that has anomalous elements within the picture that are the result of a camera defect or other natural occurrence. There are many pictures scattered about the internet that claim to be of true paranormal activity, but in fact they are "false positives." Orbs, defined as anomalous paranormal energy that can show up as balls of light or streaks in still photography or video, are the most controversial pictures of paranormal energy in the field. There are so many theories (good and bad) about the origin of orbs and what they are. Every picture in the CCPRS collection that has an orb—or orbs—are not presented in a way that state that they are absolutely paranormal of nature. I have yet to capture an orb photo that made me feel certain that in fact it is of a paranormal nature.

If you use your own camera, understand that your camera is vital. I encourage all members who own their own cameras to do research on the make and model of the camera and see what other consumers are saying about them. Does the manufacturer give any info regarding possible defects or design flaws with that particular model? Understanding your camera will help to rule out the possibility of interpreting a "false positive" for an authentic picture of paranormal activity.

Video Cameras

The video camera is also a fundamental tool in the investigation as another way for collecting objective evidence that can support the proof of paranormal activity. The video camera can be used in various ways during the investigation. It can be set on a tripod and left in a location where paranormal activity has been reported. It can also be used as a hand-held camera and the investigator will take it with them during their walk through investigation as a means of documenting to hopefully capture anomalous activity on tape. Infrared technology has become a feature on most consumer level video cameras and depending on the manufacturer can

be called "night shot" or "night alive." What this technology does is allow us to use the camera in zero light. Most cameras with this feature will add a green tint or haze to the camera when it is being used in this mode. A video camera with this ability holds great appeal to the paranormal investigator.

EMF/ELF Meters

EMF=Electro Magnetic Frequency

ELF=Extremely Low Frequency

What is an EMF/ELF meter? Good question. The EMF/ELF meter is a meter that measures Electric and Magnetic fields in an AC or DC current field. It measures in a unit of measurement called "milli-gauss," named for the famous German mathematician, Karl Gauss. Most meters will measure in a range of 1-5 or 1-10 milli-gauss. The reason that EMF meters are used in paranormal research is because of the theory that a spirit or paranormal energy can add to the energy field when it is materializing or is present in a location. The theory says that, typically, an energy that measures between 3-7 milli-gauss may be of a paranormal origin. This doesn't mean that an artificial field can't also measure within this range. That is why we take base readings and make maps notating where artificial fields occur. The artificial fields are a direct result of electricity, i.e., wiring, appliances, light switches, electrical outlets, circuit breakers, high voltage power lines, sub-stations, etc.

The Earth emits a naturally occurring magnetic field all around us and has an effect on paranormal activity. Geo-magnetic storm activity can also have a great influence on paranormal activity. For more information on this kind of phenomena visit: www. noaa.sec.com.

There are many different types of EMF meters; and each one, although it measures with the same unit of measurement, may react differently. An EMF meter can range from anywhere to $12.00 to $1,000.00 or more depending on the quality and features that it has. Most meters are measuring the AC (alternating current, the type of fields created by man-made electricity) fields and some can measure DC (direct current-naturally occurring fields, batteries also fall into the category of DC) fields. The benefit of having a meter that can measure DC fields is that they will automatically filter out the artificial fields created by AC fields and can pick up more naturally occurring electromagnetic fields. Some of the higher-tech EMF meters are so sensitive that they can pick up the fields generated by living beings. The EMF meter was originally designed to measure the earth's magnetic fields and also to measure the fields created by electrical an artificial means.

There have been various studies over the years about the long term effects of individuals living in or near high fields. There has been much controversy as to whether or not long term exposure to high fields can lead to cancer. It has been proven though that no matter what, long term exposure to high fields can be harmful to your health. The ability to locate these high fields within a private residence or business is vital to the investigation. We may offer suggestions to the client as to possible solutions for dealing with high fields. The wiring in a home or business can greatly affect the possibility of high fields. If the wiring is old and/or not shielded correctly, it can emit high fields that may affect the ability to correctly notate any anomalous fields that may be present.

Audio Recording Equipment

Audio recording equipment is used for conducting EVP (Electronic Voice Phenomena) research and experiments. What is an EVP? An EVP is a phenomenon where paranormal voices or sounds can be captured with audio recording devices. The theory is that the activity will imprint directly onto the device or tape, but has not been proven to be an absolute fact. The use of an external microphone is essential when conducting EVP experiments with analog recording equipment. The internal microphone on an analog tape recorder can pick up the background noise of the working parts within the tape recorder and can taint the evidence as a whole. Most digital recorders are quiet enough to use the internal microphone, but as a general rule of thumb, we do not use them. An external microphone will be used always. Another theory about EVP research is that an authentic EVP will happen within the range 250-400hz. This is a lower frequency range and isn't easily heard by the human ear, and the human voice does not emit in this range. EVP is rarely heard at the moment it happens—it is usually revealed during the playback and analysis portion of the investigation.

Thermometers

The use of a thermometer in an investigation goes without saying. This is how we monitor the temperature changes during the course of an investigation. CCPRS is currently using Digital thermometers with remote sensors as a way to set up a perimeter and to notate any changes in a stationary location of an investigation. The Air-probe thermometer can take "real time" readings that are instantly accurate. This is the more appropriate thermometer for measuring air temperature and "cold spots" that may be caused by the presence of paranormal phenomena. The IR Non-contact thermometer is the most misused thermometer in the field of paranormal research. CCPRS does not own or use IR Non-contact thermometers for this reason. The IR (infrared) Non-contact thermometer is meant for measuring surface temperatures from a remote location. It shoots an infrared beam out to an object and bounces to the unit and gives the temperature reading. I have seen, first hand, investigators using this thermometer as a way to measure air temperature. NO, this is not correct! There are now a variety of true air probe thermometers available on the market that has replaced the need for anyone to ever use an IR non-contact thermometer.

Mark Sarro

BATTLE TIMELINE

June 28th 1863 – General Meade's army reached Emmitsburg-New Windsor, PA

June 30th 1863 – Meade formed 3 corps, the first, third and eleventh. He placed General Reynolds in command.

June 30th – July 1st (Evening) 70,000 troops were in camp within a few miles of Gettysburg. 27,000 Union and 43,000 Confederate.

Day 1: Wednesday July 1st, 1863

Early Morning – Chambersburg Turnpike, 1.5 miles west of Gettysburg, the first shots were fired and a skirmish would soon turn into a battle.

10:30am – General Reynolds and two brigades of the Union First Corps arrive and join the battle along McPherson Ridge. General Reynolds is killed; General Doubleday takes command of the Union First Corps.

11am – Two divisions of the Union Eleventh Corps arrive north of town.

2pm – A division of General Ewell arrives and attacks the right flank of the Union First Corps.

2:10pm – General Lee arrives to meet Heth getting ready for another offensive.

2:15pm – A 2nd division of Ewell attacks the Eleventh Corps position.

3pm – At the site of the Eternal Light Peace Memorial, Confederate General Rhode's division launches an attack with a total of five brigades. This is by far the largest division in either army.

4pm – Early's division of Ewell's Corps enter from the northeast on Harrisburg Road and cause the right flank of the Eleventh Corps to give way. This sets off a chain reaction down the two-mile Union line. The First and Eleventh Corps retreat to Cemetery Hill and Culp's Hill. General Howard had saved a third division to fortify Cemetery Hill in the case of retreat.

5pm – The Confederates seem to have won the battle. General Lee wants to ensure victory and instructs Ewell to attack Cemetery Hill as needed. Ewell does not attack.

Day 2: Thursday July 2nd, 1863

Shortly after midnight – General Meade arrives and decides to figtht from a strong defensive position.

Just before dawn – Most of the Rebel Army of Northern Virginia arrive in Gettysburg except for General Stuart's and Longstreet's corps, General Pickett's division, and General Law's Brigade. They arrive later that day after marching all night.

4pm – Longstreet's troops attack with Law's brigade at the lead. Union Army Chief of engineers General Warren sounds the attack so that General Vincent moves his men in place on Little Round Top. The 20th Maine, led by Colonel Chamberlain, is positioned on the left side.

The Wheatfield Battle continues for three hours while the Confederates take Rose Farm, The Peach Orchard, The Wheatfield, Trostle Farm, and Devil's Den.

7pm – In a last ditch effort of defense, Colonel Chamberlain gives the order for Bayonets and they charge down the hill into Confederate lines.

8pm – The Confederates remain in control of the Peach Orchard, the Wheatfield, Trostle farm, and Devil's Den, and through the night, they take control of Spangler's Spring.

General Greene's brigade, along with General Johnson's division, clash with two brigades of Early's division at Cemetery Hill and Culp's Hill as dusk approaches.

Overnight – The Confederate Pickett's division arrives with Stuart's three cavalry brigades. The Union side General Sedwick's Sixth Corps arrive. General Meade takes a vote from his generals and they decide to stay and fight.

Day 3: Friday July 3ᴿᴰ 1863

4:30am – Union troops continue to fight at Culp's Hill which lasts for almost seven hours.

8:30am – The Sniper fire between Confederate troops in town and Union troops on Cemetery Hill cause the one and only civilian casualty; Jennie Wade is shot and killed by a stray bullet that enters through two doors and strikes her in the kitchen while making bread.

1pm – The Confederate Stuart's cavalry attach the rear of the Union line that includes General Custer at Cemetery Ridge.

Cannon shots are fired from Seminary Ridge; this signals the Confederates to increase the intensity of the attack near the copse of trees on Cemetery Ridge. The Union side strikes back with nearly two hours of continuous fire from 250 cannons.

2-3pm – The Confederates ammunition runs low. General Pickett asks Longstreet whether he should advance; Pickett's Charge begitns.

4pm – General Armistad and almost 200 men make it through the angle in the stone wall; mortally wounded, he places his hand on an enemy cannon to signify he captures it. The Confederates would not advance any further and those who survive Pickett's charge retreat in defeat.

5pm – Union cavalry division commander General Kilpatrick learns of the defeat and launches a counterattack west of the Round Top hills; he is unsuccessful.

BIBLIOGRAPHY

Haskell, Franklin Aretas and Col. Frank Haskel. *The Battle of Gettysburg – The Eyewitness Account*, Chapman Billies Inc.: Sandwich MA. 1993.

Lee, Anthony W. and Elizabeth Young. *Gardner's Photographic Sketch Book of the Civil War*, Dover Publications Inc.: New York, NY. 1959.

Roseberry, D. P. *Ghosts of Valley Forge and Phoenixville*. Schiffer Publishing Ltd.: Atglen, PA 2006.

Stackpole, Edward J. *They Met at Gettysburg*. Stackpole Books: Mechanicsburg PA. 1956.

Sarro, Mark. *Ghosts of West Chester*. Schiffer Publishing: Atglen, PA 2008.

Sarro, Mark and Michelle Rainey. *CCPRS Handbook*. CCPRS Books: West Chester PA. 19382 Copyright 2006

Thomas, Dean S. The Confederate Field Manual. (Reprinted from the 1862 edition), Unknown Publisher: Gettysburg, PA. New material copyright 1984.

WEB RESOURCES

CCPRS (Chester County Paranormal Research Society). www.chestercountyprs.com.

Joe Svehla, Ghostly Images. www.ghosttour.net/gettysburg.html

Laurie Hull, Delaware County Paranormal Research. www.delco-ghosts.com.

Para-X Radio Network. www.para-x.com

The ITC Lounge. www.mogulus.com/itclounge

Voices Carry Paranormal Radio, www.voicescarryradio.com

www.visit-gettysburg.com

PLACES INDEX